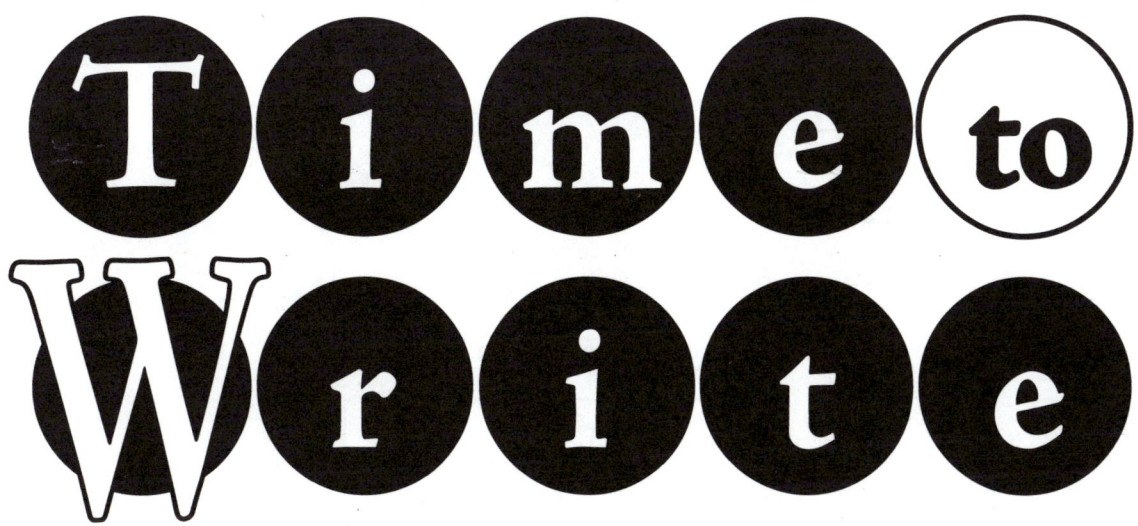

Robin Johnson

Book Five: Grade Three

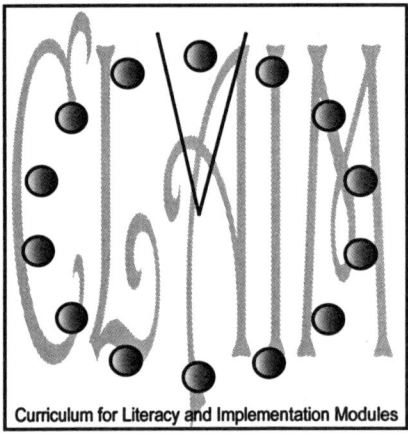

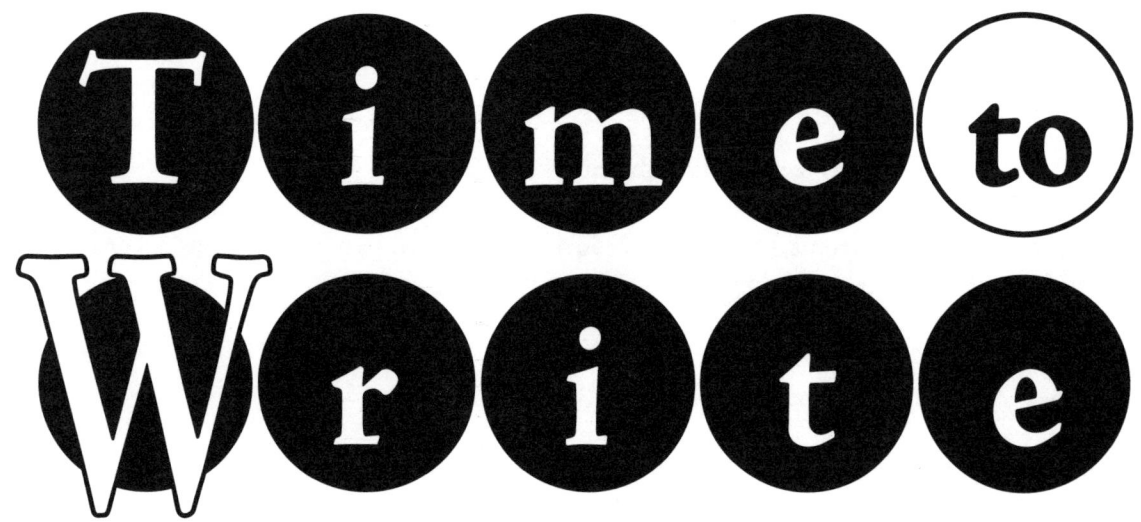

Robin Johnson

foreword by
Susan Stevens Crummel

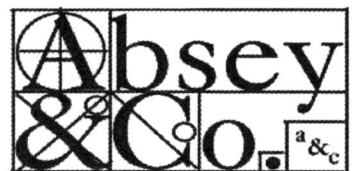

Spring, TX ♦ New York

Copyright © 2008 Robin Johnson

All rights reserved. No part of this publication may be
reproduced, transmitted, or stored in an information retrieval system in any form or by any
means, graphic, electronic, or mechanical, including photocopying, taping, and recording
without prior written permission from the publisher.

Library of Congress Control Number: 2008923840

ISBN 978-1-888842-53-1

Printed in the United States of America

Requests for permission to make copies
of any part of the work should be mailed to:

Permissions
Absey & Co. Inc.
23011 Northcrest
Spring, Texas 77389

Visit us at www.Absey.biz

To my mom, Linda, my first teacher, and the one who taught me to always smile and always believe.

To my children, Caleb and Sophie, who teach me how to experience the world through the eyes of a child again.

And to my husband, David, for putting up with my many hours on the computer and the stacks of children's work that covered our living room.

Thank you to Joyce and Eddie, along with the other members of the CoMission and the Abydos trainers who have encouraged me along the way and taught me what I know. I am a better person because of meeting and learning from each of you.

Table of Contents

Foreword—viii
Preface—ix
Introduction—1
Chapter 1—Time to Get Ready—2
Chapter 2—Time in a Day—6
Chapter 3—Time to Engage in the Process—8
Chapter 4—Time to Start—13
Chapter 5—In Twenty-one Days Time—16
Chapter 6—The Rest of the Time—31
Chapter 7—Time to Connect—46
Chapter 8—Time for Everything Else—57
Chapter 9—Assessment Time—63
Chapter 10—Moments in Time—65
Chapter 11—Time Is on Our Side—68
Appendix A—69
References—70

Foreword

Teaching kids is like doing laundry. You start off with a huge pile of clothes—disheveled, unsorted, some items soiled more than others, and many with no washing instructions. Slowly you begin to work through the pile, washing a few on the normal cycle, a few on the gentle cycle, but most on the heavy duty cycle. Some are easy care and come out with no wrinkles. Some you have to iron and iron and still the creases show. Then, after you have whittled away the entire pile and are patting yourself on the back proclaiming that the laundry is DONE, you turn around and a whole new pile awaits you. It's fall again.

So why do we teach? Because teaching is a noble profession? (We think so, but does anyone else?) Because we want to make a difference? (Possibly.) Because over the summer we forget the pain? (Getting closer.) Because we are nuts? (That's it!)

But there is a special breed of teachers. You know them by the dazed look in their eyes. They are gluttons for punishment. They are the ones who get to teach the third graders how to write coherently, effectively, and creatively. They have the biggest, hardest, scariest laundry pile of all.

This book is like a light in the tunnel for those teachers. Robin Johnson, an innovative writing teacher and NJWPT/Abydos trainer, has illuminated the way with fun yet concrete ways to make writing an integral part of every school day. Her literature-based approach is guaranteed to hook the kids so they can see that writing is fun, not a chore. And I bet it will make teachers see that doing the laundry is not such a chore, either!

So get down off of your IVORY towers! If you want to see a GAIN in scores, stem the TIDE of apathy about writing, and add CHEER to every day, then use this book! You don't have to SURF around—it's ALL right here!

Susan Stevens Crummel

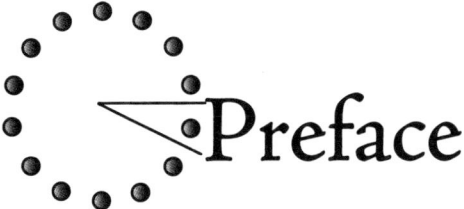

Preface

CLAIM: Curricular Literacy and Implementation Modules

In March of 2004, following the NJWPT (now Abydos Learning International) Teachers' and Trainers' Annual Conference, where influential Board of Directors of Abydos Site Directors continued to point out the one gap in the project was implementation, we began work to establish a CO-MISSION of trainers who would represent grades Pre-K through 12. We declared it a "CO" mission, not a "Commission" because we wanted to emphasize its work as one with an equality of purpose.

Invitational letters were sent to fourteen handpicked NJWPT/Abydos Trainers for this important goal. All accepted. With us as directors, we referred to this group as CO-MISSION SIXTEEN. Sixteen of us made it our mission to help young, in-coming, inexperienced teachers and those who loved the institute but who were in a quandary about exactly how to implement it, work it into their stated curricula, or integrate the project's principles, strategies, and philosophy into their day-to-day classroom agenda.

Our initial meeting, held September 4, 2004 at the Hotel Sofitel in Houston, boasted a core group of enthusiastic trainers representing thirteen disparate districts across the state. Since we all agreed our purpose centered on the importance of implementation, we tackled how to research, design, and launch this mission. We asked ourselves: What common sources could we all read? What would be the best way to share our collective expertise? How best could we share our methods of implementation? What title might we use for our work?

After grappling with a host of acronyms ranging from CLIMB: A Curriculum for Literacy Implementation and Model Building to ACCLAIM: A Content Curriculum for Literacy and Implementation Model to our favorite CLIP: A Curriculum Implementation Plan, we dismissed some for negative connotations, others were "taken," still others we felt were not quite on target with our mission, and a few were too cumbersome or wordy. This terrific group of CO-MISSION members finally unanimously chose CLAIM: Curricular Literacy and Implementation Modules.

We liked that the word claim suggested ownership, something we wanted each teacher to experience, grab on to, and hold. We liked the specificity of the words literacy and implementation. We really liked the word modules, suggesting standards, dimensionality, the sense of interchangeability, as well as units of instruction.

We brainstormed and researched and finalized the following sources for all of us to read:

Caine, Renate Nummela and Geoffrey Caine. Education on the Edge of Possibility. Alexandria, VA: ASCD, 1997.

Glickman, Carl. "Pretending Not to Know What We Know." Educational Leadership, 48 (8) 4-10, 1991.

Hall, Gene E. and Shirley M. Hord. Implementing Change. Boston: MA: Allyn & Bacon, 2005.

Jersild, Arthur T. When Teachers Face Themselves. NY: Teachers
College Press, 1995.

Joyce, B. and Showers, B. "Improving Inservice Training: the Message
of Research." Educational Leadership, 37 (5), 379-385, 1980.

So we had self-imposed homework to do.

We envisioned a series with a book for each level written by teachers who teach and implement NJWPT/Abydos on that level. We decided to engage colleagues to share in this process through input, feedback, and support. We also wanted to produce videos (still a possibility) so teachers could see implementation in action. To that end, and perhaps ambitiously, we invited a tech expert to our next meeting.

Between 2004 and the first phase of publishing, we met at least once in the summer, several times at the NJWPT/Abydos retreat, and always at the conference. In between these times, cadres met. For example, the Pre-K through first grade met, or the third, fourth, and fifth grades met.

Then we hit our first snag.

The trainer committed to write the twelve grade book moved—not just districts but out of state. We had to find another trainer. Then it happened again. This time the trainer committed to the ninth grade book entered law school. We had to find another trainer. A third trainer became a principal, and although she maintained her commitment, her new position impinged upon her time. A fourth took a position in another district as a curriculum coordinator, but she had worked ahead of time and actually was the first trainer to complete her book.

We were flexible. Deadlines came and went—and we realized our desire to have thirteen books published in one year, thirteen books to be launched at a single conference was not to be. So we regrouped and decided to introduce the books in phases. Phase One, then, would come out in 2008 with subsequent phases in subsequent years.

Throughout the process, we all grew. We listed possible items for the modules—twenty-two to be exact—we discussed the vocabulary of concept, strategy, activity, tactic, and we reviewed levels of lessons. We contacted parents and students for permissions, took pictures, made videos. We studied and contacted authors for Forewords, each of us sharing in the joy when one us received a letter from our "author" agreeing to write a colleague's Foreword. Some even entertained the idea of an Afterword. Most of all we remained cohesive and energized.

So after four years of study, hard work, camaraderie, and lots of writing, we offer you this book of phase one in the series CLAIM: Curricular Literacy and Implementation Modules. We hope you learn from, through, and because of it. We hope this book and this series helps you make NJWPT/Abydos come as alive in your classroom as it does in ours. We have gained so much professionally and believe we are doubly validated because our work will grow exponentially through you and your students. Know that all lives you touch directly or indirectly will be enhanced because of this undertaking.

May the process be with you......

Joyce Armstrong Carroll, Ed. D., H.L.D. Co-director, NJWPT/Abydos Learning

Series Authors:

Jimmie O'Quinn, Pre-K, Spring Branch ISD
Kim Dumaine, Kindergarten, Richardson ISD
Valerie Sosa, First, Pflugerville ISD
Natalie Hoskins, Second, Friendswood ISD
Robin Johnson, Third, Lovejoy ISD
Bobby Purcell, Fourth, Amarillo ISD
Jodi Hughes, Fifth, Austin ISD
Suzy Lockamy, Sixth, Northside ISD
Michelle Jackson, Seventh, Granbury ISD
Steve Kelly, Eighth, Edinburg ISD
Mona Robinson, Tenth, Pasadena ISD
Dottie Hall, Eleventh, Northside ISD

Introduction

"What is time? The shadow on the dial, the striking of the clock, the running of the sand, day and night, summer and winter, months, years, centuries —these are but arbitrary and outward signs, the measure of Time, not Time itself. Time is the Life of the soul."
Henry Wadsworth Longfellow

"Is it writing time yet?" "Are we having writing time today?"
When I first began implementing the teaching of writing in my classroom, I heard these questions every day. My answer was always, "Yes, of course we will write today." I couldn't understand why students would ask those questions over and over. Didn't they know we were going to write? I always let them work on their stories and share ideas. What I didn't understand then was that I had made writing "time" only about lessons and the teaching of writing. The students saw it as an hour in the day where I would teach something specifically about writers and in the remaining time give them freedom to enjoy their own writing "time." In the ensuing years of teaching writing, I realized the many ways to model and show students what good writing looks like, but more importantly, our writing time expanded, happening all day long, in every subject, for every experience. Writing time is "all of the time."

Time is one of those words that has different meanings for different people depending on the context. In the case of my students' questions, *time* meant a specific moment in the day: a number on the clock, an hour with our pencils. For many, including myself as a third-grade teacher, *time* is something that we do not feel we have enough of: a measure of hurriedness and "getting it all done." As I prepared for this book, I e-mailed over one hundred third-grade teachers to ask them about writing in their classrooms. The number one complaint was, "I don't have enough time!" With paperwork, other subjects and assessment areas to cover, high-stakes testing, special classes, and even lunch, there just does not seem to be adequate time in the day to do it all. It seems to be a universal problem.

So, my goal in writing this book is to demonstrate how I managed to change my students' view of their writing time; they no longer ask me the "when" question because it's no longer about the hour of the day, it's about the expression of ideas and communication on paper. It is about "having time" and "making time" to write all the time.

1 Time To Get Ready

"To choose time is to save time." Sir Francis Bacon

I don't remember ever thinking of myself as a writer until I took the New Jersey Writing Project in Texas/Abydos Learning summer institute eight years ago. Even after two years of teaching, I still felt like a new teacher and at times was still doing what everyone else told me to do. In my classroom, we wrote on worksheets, in a journal if we had time, or practiced handwriting. It was just something we did to get our answers down on the paper. The three-week institute changed that. For the first time I created writing for myself and for others. I had family stories to tell, experiences to share, and new ways to communicate. My life and my memories were a part of a history that had never been written down. Writing became an outlet for my emotions and the words I was too afraid to say out loud. I wanted to take that feeling of euphoria back to my students and help them feel like writers too.

As the summer wound down, I began thinking about my classroom and getting it prepared for the first day. The layout of my room has always been important to me, but now I knew I wanted a place for students to feel comfortable to write, have resources available for writing, and a space for supplies; I had to rethink where it all would go. I realized that an inviting writing environment begins with having materials ready and available to use the first time you write.

Our Writing Center

I have one shelf (Fig.1.1) that has traveled with me from room to room where I keep all my community writing supplies and resources for my students to use. I try to have a table (Fig. 1.2) near the shelf for more space as well. These are the items I have for my students on that shelf:

- thesaurus,
- dictionaries,
- pencils,
- erasers,
- pens in black and other colors,
- stickers,
- red cups,
- notebook paper,

Fig. 1.1

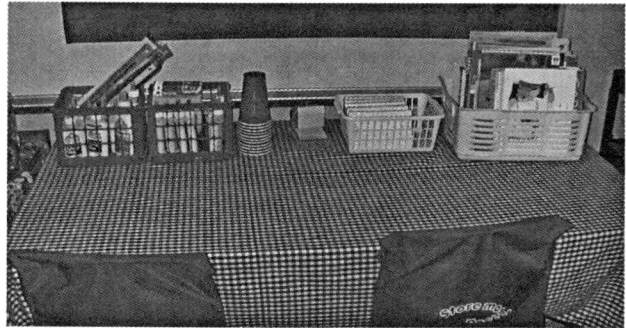
Fig. 1.2

Fig. 1.3

- white paper,
- construction paper.

I also keep two large white buckets on the top of the shelf (Fig. 1.3). One holds poetry books and the other holds books about authors and the writing process.

Our Supplies

On the supply list, my students bring the things I know we will use to keep our writing organized:
- 5 pocket folders without brads,
- two single subject spirals,
- and a three-subject spiral.

At one time, I tried to have the students bring specific colors so everything would match, but sometimes that did not happen. I also bought folders and spirals myself one year, but that was expensive. I decided colors were not important to the writing, and we could label the supplies clearly enough so that students would know exactly which ones they were to use. In past years, one folder was not large enough to hold everything, so it became messy; multiple loose folders got confusing and misplaced. I had to come up with a way to put everything in one place. The five-pocket folders, bound together to become one folder, has helped my students have access to a resource at their desk that holds everything. Each student has his or her own and claims ownership. I have premade labels ready, either typed on the computer or handwritten, to save time at the beginning of the year. This seems a daunting task at first, but in the long run proves a valuable timesaver for teaching writing. Each folder opens up with the two labeled pockets inside. The students understand the use of each folder when I explain what each label means.

Fig. 1.4

The outside of the folder is labeled "(Student's Name)'s Writing Tools" (Fig. 1.4). This becomes a place to store minilesson notes, ideas, charts, and checklists that we do together.

On the first folder, the left side label is "Things We Can Write About" (Fig. 1.5) which will contain student and teacher generated lists of topics and reflexive subjects gathered from minilessons. The right side label is "Prewriting and Ideas" where we add prewriting strategies we have tried throughout the year. The second folder's left side reads " Words I

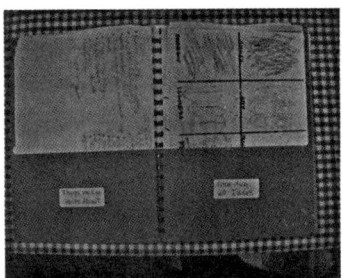

Fig. 1.5

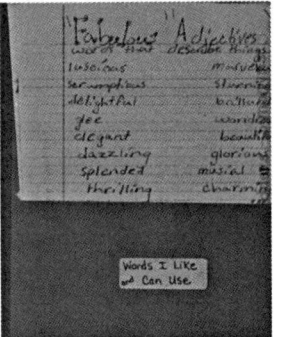

Fig. 1.6

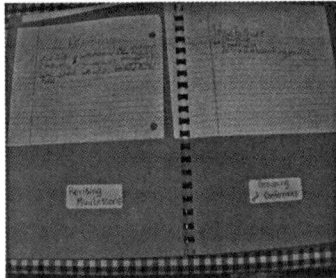

Fig. 1.7

Fig. 1.8

Like and Can Use" (Fig. 1.6). This folder houses words they hear or see in books we read, words they think they would like to use in their writing. It also contains vocabulary lessons. The right side reads "Poetry" and becomes the place for examples of poetry we read in class or the students find or write on their own.

The third folder's left side reads "Revising Minilessons" which is anything I teach to help them reenter and rework their writing, the right side reads "Grouping and Conferences" (Fig 1.7).

The fourth folder's left side, containing grammar and mechanics lessons, is labeled "Editing Minilessons and Checklist." Its right side, "Word Wall and Spelling," holds strategies for spelling, patterns we have covered and high frequency words.

The fifth folder's left side contains "Ways to Publish" with a list of genres and types of written products. "Pieces I've Published" (Fig. 1.8), a compilation of works, is on the right side.

For the students' actual writing, whether journaling, quick writes, connections, or pieces they have started, I use the one subject writing spiral. This is their "Writer's Notebook." Third-grade students stop and start many pieces of writing here, so it is a place for all of their beginnings, endings, and everything in between. We date each page. Sometimes a writing lesson we do together prompts a story that interrupts the pages of a piece the students have begun days before. In that instance, I model how students can put a symbol at the bottom of one page and then add that same symbol to another page where they may continue the same piece. The titling of pages and ideas helps the students easily organize their unfinished pieces or quickly find an idea they want to pursue in a future draft.

Additionally, because we write throughout the day, we have in our supplies a "Learning Log," or a three subject spiral, that holds our content writing in math, science, and social studies.

Displaying Our Work

"Publishing is the heart of children's writing" another NJWPT/Abydos trainer once told me. As I watched my students write and write and write that first year, I knew that was true.

Children want to feel ownership and see their work displayed. They are proud of what they have written. So I make sure I have plenty of space in the hallway and around the room for the children to display their work. Each year, I create a catchy bulletin board title, the first one is "Publishing Is the Heart of Children's Writing." Bulletin boards can be time consuming unless you allow the students to have control of what they want to display. I start the year off with the background paper up, the title words written, and a spot for each child's writing. They do the rest. As soon as they have a piece of writing that they want to show or a paper they have worked hard on ready to go up, they put it in its spot. Under the quote "Publishing Is the Heart of Children's Writing," each child writes his or her name on a heart, then affixes his or her writing to a different colored sheet of construction paper with a paper clip. One year, we used a lesson I always do from the poem, "The Butterfly Jar" by Jeff Moss, as the focus of our display. The children decorated butterflies and we hot glued them to clothes pins, spaced the clothes pins out on rick rack, and stapled that to the wall.

Fig. 1.9

Fig. 1.10

I like using a play on words for titles of publishing spots. On one wall, I placed a bench and a fake ficus tree. Above this wall, I wrote, *Look What We're Learning! Come and See, Sit and Relax Under Our "Poet" Tree!* I have also used Dr. Seuss inspired titles, such as "Oh the Places Our Stories Can Go in Third Grade" or "My Many Colored Stories" At times throughout the year, I staple a folder of index cards to the wall near the students' work, and a sheet of instructions so other students or teachers may stop and write positive comments and encouragement about a piece of writing they have read. My first years of teaching, I stressed over the bulletin boards; I wanted them to match the season, look perfect, and each week meant a completely new bulletin board. Now I know that what matters most is honoring the writing that the students are producing every day.

Besides student work, we also have charts that we make together to act as memory aids during writing time. If there is space, charts are stapled in a row on an empty wall. I have also hung the charts on a chart stand with hangers or on hangers placed on a hook protruding from a cabinet on the wall. Then the students may pull the chart they need. The information on these "anchor" charts (Fig. 1.11) may also be added to the "Writer's Tools" folders if a student needs them when writing outside the classroom.

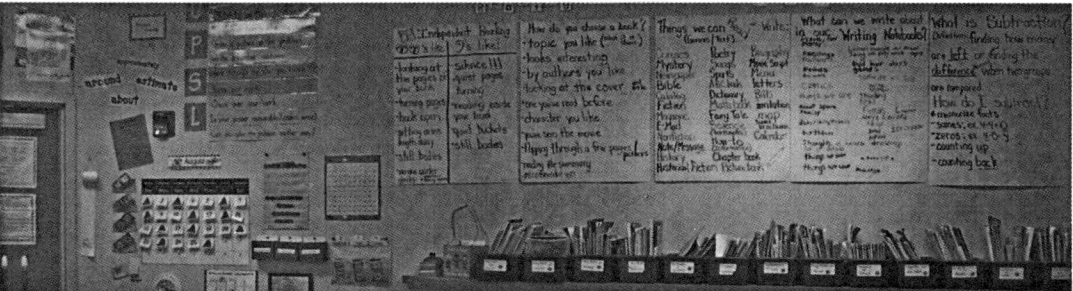
Fig. 1.11

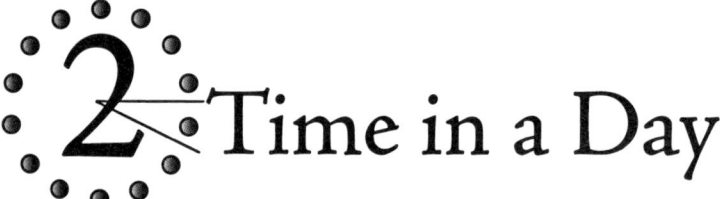
Time in a Day

"The bad news is time flies. The good news is you're the pilot."
Michael Althsuler

"There is not enough time in a day." Over and over I hear that from teachers and many times think it myself. But, as I have heard said before and firmly believe, "You don't have enough time NOT to write." Because writing can be done within any subject or about any topic, it can and must be done every day. Consistency and daily writing makes the difference between students feeling like they are writers and just thinking they can write. In *The Art of Teaching Writing*, Lucy Calkins points out that it is almost impossible to create an effective writing workshop if students only write once or twice a week (188). She elaborates with the importance of setting aside a predictable time for writing each day (185). In Chapters Six through Eight, I elaborate on how I integrate writing into other subject areas during the day, but here I want to focus on how I schedule my writing "time" for the types of writing we do.

Our Writing Workshop

I call the time of day when students engage in the writing process, working on their own stories and pieces, or writing from ideas generated in their writer's notebooks, "writing workshop." I begin with a minilesson. Minilessons are usually short, fifteen to twenty minutes of modeling what I, as a writer, do, such as, looking at another author's work, or learning concrete ways for students to reenter, reworking writing. My writing workshop usually lasts at least an hour per day. The hour consists of the fifteen minute minilesson, thirty minutes of student writing and conferencing time, and fifteen minutes of share time. That may seem neat and tidy, but it is quite flexible.

Other Times to Write

Every subject area lends itself to writing, either through fact finding, processing information, or reflection. My day may include a fifteen minute time of writing in a math journal, "What does addition mean to you and when do you use it?" or it may be explaining in that same journal the steps the student uses to solve a word problem. It also may include time to reflect on the science experiment we just completed or time to rewrite in their own words the experiment to take home and try with parents. Incorporating writing throughout the day shows students how their writing can take different forms and doesn't always have to be about writing an original story.

My Schedule

Every year my schedule changes. I am required to have a ninety minute math block, a minimum of two hours for the language arts block; the other content areas get sandwiched

> **Daily Schedule**
>
> 8:00–9:30 Math Block
> 9:30 – 10:00 Independent Reading Block
> 10:00 – 10:45 Specials / Break
> 10:45 – 11:45 Instructional Reading Block
> 11:45 – 12:40 Science or Social Studies
> 12:40 – 1:10 Lunch
> 1:10 – 1:40 Working with Words Block
> (spelling, editing, vocabulary)
> 1:40 – 2:40 Writing Workshop

in between. This year, my day looked like this:

Because I have such a big chunk of time at the end of the day and the students are usually tired, I have placed my writing block there. The students love it, have some freedom of movement and sharing, and are excited about the end of the day. I am too. With my reading and content areas close together, I can be flexible and move lessons around if I need to or integrate when appropriate. Some days, my writing workshop time is my big chunk of writing and some days we do our biggest chunk of writing during reading or Science. Either way works, as long as the students are writing every day!

Writing is our primary form of communication during the day whether it is to teach each other or to teach ourselves.

3 Time to Engage in the Process

"Time is a dressmaker specializing in alterations."
Faith Baldwin

What I have experienced most as I worked through my own writing is the recursive nature of the process (Carroll & Wilson 66, 85). The process does not happen for each student in the same way at the same time. It is important to teach in minilessons what may happen during each stage of the process during writing workshop. Students engage in the parts of the process as they work on their own pieces while I model and explain. Students understand when they write on their own that the stages of the process flow in and out of each other as needed. They may have gained a starting point through prewriting, but as they draft they may edit or cross out, and then realize they need to do some more prewriting or draft and revise more.

I show students pieces of my own writing from beginning to end. They see the scratch outs, changes in directions, and the pages it took to get to the final piece. I know that for many teachers this flexibility is hard to imagine in a classroom of twenty or more students. In Chapter 2, I explain how I manage writing workshop, including time management, students engaging in all stages of the process at once, and the teacher's role.

In *Acts of Teaching*, the components of the writing process are identified as prewriting, writing, postwriting, editing, and publishing, with postwriting subdivided into correcting, revising, and reformulating (Carroll & Wilson 30). To streamline the process for third-graders, I use the terms prewriting, drafting, revising, editing, and publishing. I have included conferencing and sharing in this chapter because both are so important to help students when they get stuck. Each of the stages of the process require scaffolding where I model what processes writers encounter as they think, write, and plan. Sometimes I do this on a chart or an overhead; other times I use the pages of a children's book. Then I work jointly with the students through conferencing and collaboration. Scaffolding writers as they work through the writing process supports Vygotsky's theory that "What a child can do in cooperation today he can do alone tomorrow" (Carroll & Wilson 317).

Prewriting

In *Clearing the Way: Working With Teenage Writers*, Tom Romano refers to prewriting as "percolating" (56). The "drip, drip, drip" of thoughts and ideas that flow from my students doesn't happen just because I say it is time to write. Ideas can come any minute, in any place. My students need to be prepared to capture those percolations as they come. I tell my students that I have used torn napkins, the backs of bank receipts, and scraps of envelopes to hold the musings that have come to me without warning and without preparation, but many of these words and images have gotten lost over the years because they were mistaken for trash. So that their words will never get thrown out, my students have the option to carry their writer's notebook with them wherever they go, including to the restroom, on field trips, to lunch, and definitely when they go home, or not. Students soon learn that having the freedom of their spiral with them allows them to capture their prewriting wherever they go, so they don't worry about whether they will forget anything during writing workshop.

Prewriting minilessons help students think of ideas, trigger memories, or make connections. Prewriting signals the beginnings of any writing they will ever do. So the choices of prewriting strategies we practice through our minilessons are easily accessible throughout the year. I start the first week of school listing them on an ongoing anchor chart to display on the classroom wall while students create a similar list in their folder of "Writing Tools" (Fig. 3.1).

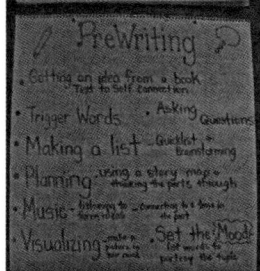

Fig. 3.1

Drafting

Drafting is the time in the process where I tell students to "write like the wind," without fear of mistakes or failure. I go over a few hints that help make the drafting stage easier for them. This includes skipping lines, writing on only one side of the page, using a black pen, and crossing one line through a word instead of erasing. They may not understand these strategies until I have modeled the entire process. Then they see that when writers revise and edit, they need space on the paper for additions and changes. I show them that if I erase a word, it is gone from the page forever, and I may not be able to retrieve it again. We make another anchor chart as a memory aid, but these ways to draft do not come naturally at first. It is okay if they forget. I simply remind them to start where they are on the page and keep going. As they mature in their process, leaving room to rework will be more important to them. At first, I encourage the draft in whatever form it takes.

Revising

As a writer myself, the revising stage of the process is the most integrated for me. I cross out as I write, change words, go back and forth with ideas, and rethink. This way of revision came with practice and time spent writing. I had to learn ways I could revise because I was like a child who thought my paper was "done" the first time. Revision lessons have to do with changing the content of the paper. I have learned that many times the best way to encourage students to revise is through conferencing, sharing individually or in small groups.

Conferences

Conferences, whether with peers or with me, can happen at any and all stages of the process. Talking to someone may trigger a new idea or a change in the writing students are working on at that moment. Carl Anderson in *How's It Going?* says conferences "are the heart of workshop teaching"(2). They are conversations between writers. Conferences happen in my classroom during the student writing portion of writing workshop. A red cup from my writing center sitting on a student's desk signals that the student wants or needs a conference. I always try to move to the student for a conference (Fig. 3.2). This saves time and keeps the room quiet. If a student has not signaled me to conference in a few days time, I move my conference stool to that student anyway.

Fig. 3.2

Documentation is one of the keys to conferencing. I keep a record of each student with whom I conference, and a note or two to remind me of our topic of conversation. This record stays on my clipboard that moves along with me. The conference record helps me see at a glance what students are working on and who I need to meet with that day. (See Appendix A—Writing Workshop Documentation Log.) My first question vacillates between, "How's it going?" and "What are you working on today?" If a student is not really sure, I prompt with, "What would you like show me or read to me from your writing?" At first, I thought I needed to hear a student's entire piece to be able to help, but if I want to meet with more than one student a day, I have to use the conference time wisely, get straight to the area of need, and choose one topic to focus on in a three to five minute span (Anderson 18). If I do not watch myself, this can turn in to a time of teaching instead of guiding the student along. If I see that many of the students are struggling with the same issue, then I pull them together for a quick micro-mini-teach (Carroll, *Authentic*, 8). I am able to make decisions about future lessons that the whole class needs when I am conferencing because I often see a concept many students are missing.

Fig. 3.3

Besides conferencing with me, the students conference with each other. (Fig. 3.3) Over the years I have seen a greater need for structure in these peer conferences so that the students use their time wisely and well. In the first few weeks of school, I teach a lesson on what a conference looks like, what types of questions you can ask each other, and how to be a good listener. One anchor chart we make together consists of a list of conferencing prompts we can ask ourselves or each other, such as: I like the part about…, I would like to know more about…, I wonder about…, I don't understand this part…, and What happens after…. Modeling is the best way to ensure positive starts to student conferencing.

I have a recording sheet students must fill out before they peer conference. It includes the name of the student requesting the conference and the student's name that they would like to conference with that day. The writer must also include his or her reasons for needing a conference. If time is an issue with some students, I have them write the time the conference started and the time it ended. This record keeping is another type of writing experience students encounter in my classroom and in the world.

I let the students know when their conference request is granted and they, with practice, also become familiar with gauging the time spent with the other person. This structure keeps both my students and me on track and gives us enough time to write and discuss within our writing workshop time.

Group Strategies

Putting the students into groups gives me a chance to be inventive and have a little fun. I want grouping to be random so the students gain insight from different writers and hear multiple pieces of writing. I have used stickers, playing cards, paper with the four seasons written on them, matching pictures, socks, earrings, and numbers to put the students in their groups. I try to keep groups to no more than five students. This allows all students to have a chance to read their piece and respond to other pieces, while receiving feedback from more students than usual. Time does not allow us to group every day, but because of the benefits, I make sure we group at least once every two weeks. I do it on the day where I have the most time in my schedule because grouping can take from thirty to forty-five minutes.

I teach two main grouping strategies throughout the year: *Pointing* and *Say Back* (Carroll & Wilson 151). Both of these strategies include having the writer read his or her piece twice. With third graders that creates an atmosphere of better listening. Some students can only concentrate on one instruction at a time, so they listen for enjoyment first and then during the second reading, they write down the information to share with the writer. To their group share time, they take their piece of writing, sticky notes to write on, and a pencil.

In *Pointing*, the listeners "point out" a word or phrase that they liked. I start with this technique because it contains nothing but positive feedback and helps students become comfortable with the riskiness of sharing their writing.

I move to *Say Back* later to provide students with a strategy for revising and adding to their writing but still in a positive environment. During *Say Back*, listeners write down what they liked and then what they want to know more about, a question they have, or a part they didn't understand (Carroll & Wilson 157). We may do the same strategies three or four times, but then students have the choice to use that strategy at any time in their one-on-one peer conferences. Once again we make an anchor chart that names the strategy and gives its procedures.

Editing

The editing stage of the process deals with what we usually call the mechanics of writing: capitalization, punctuation, spelling, sentence composition, and grammar. Using the skills required by the state along with my students needs, I plan editing lessons. Editing must be taught through the use of the students' own writing. For example, in third grade my students have learned many of the rules for capitalization. I often reteach those rules, such as capitalizing the beginning of a sentence or a name, and then I invite the students to go back into their pieces looking for places where they should have followed those rules but didn't.

Spelling is a subject that needs to be taught within the students' writing. I teach spelling through the use of patterns and high frequency words. Our brain connects letters and words for us through words we already know. So, if my students learn to spell *back*, they are able to spell *stack, track, black,* and *crack*. The problem is that many words in the English language don't follow a pattern; those words we call high frequency words, such as *friend, they,* and *because*. Each week I teach five new high frequency words that I have noticed my students missing in their writing. We add those to a "Word Wall" that stays up in the room all year.

We learn the four spelling rules, "doubling consonants, changing *y* to *I*, dropping the final *e* before suffixes, and writing *i* before *e* except after *c*" and keep a reference in our writing tools folder for use during writing time (Carroll & Wilson 201). Editing rules can not be simply told to the students one day and then expected to be mastered by the next. Students must apply the rules consistently and repeatedly, after modeling, with guidance and then on their own. (Fig. 3.4)

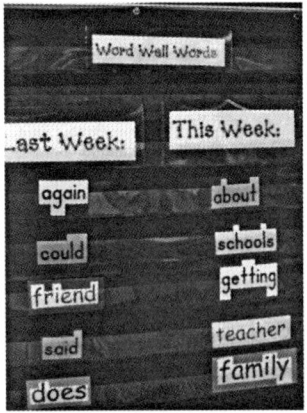

Fig. 3.4

Fig. 3.5

Publishing

Many teachers assume that publishing can only be done with pictures and bound books. They dismiss this part of the process because it takes too long. Publishing is the finished piece of writing, the stage where the students are ready to give the piece up and turn it over to someone else. Sometimes that takes the form of a bound book, a typed paper, or a neatly written final copy. At the beginning of third grade especially, students want to illustrate everything. Once again the time management part of writing workshop becomes an issue. I have one computer in my classroom, so it is not feasible for all students to use it. We have access to the computer lab once a week and many students type then. Many times, a student decides to take his or her paper home to complete this part of the process. When students desire to illustrate their pieces, I allow them two days of writing workshop to use at school. They can then finish the drawings at home or during a free moment. I have found this to be the best way to continue their daily flow of writing without too much interruption. I keep track of their publishing time on the same conference record I use at other stages in the process.

Author's Chair

Part of the publishing stage of the writing process extends to the Author's Chair. This is a special place for the students to sit, such as a rocking chair or director's chair, to share their published pieces. This share chair awaits students and their writing in the front of the room. Even though we share some part of our writing every day, either from the minilesson or workshop time, students need to know that when they finish a piece, they earn the spotlight and time of celebration. (Fig. 3.5)

4 Time to Start

"Take time to deliberate, but when the time for action arrives, stop thinking and go in."
Andrew Jackson

The first day of school is the perfect time to set the writing tone for the year. Although that day is filled with collecting supplies, paperwork, procedures, and introducing the students to the room and each other, I set the expectations for our writing classroom with every student engaged in writing from day one. I start our first prewriting activity with a reading/writing connection within the first hour. Most of the students will have their spiral available, but if not, I supply the choice of another spiral or a few pieces of notebook paper. We date each new writing at the top of the page for future reference. Today, though, is not the time to worry about format or length. I want the writing atmosphere to start off positively with a relaxing and comfortable time of reading a children's book and then writing what comes naturally, what the children feel.

Many choices of books abound dealing with the first day emotions, but I choose to read *Little Cliff's First Day of School* by Clifton L. Taulbert. The main character deals with his feelings of fear, inadequacy, and lack of desire to attend school after a summer at home. The students identify with those same thoughts as they prepare for a new year. We gather around my rocking chair and I read. With their spirals out on their desk waiting, time will transition easily from listening to thinking to writing. As I close the book, we discuss what the book was about and what connections they are making to their first day. I believe that here at the beginning especially, when many of the students are still unsure of themselves, we must process our thoughts out loud before we commit them to the page. We talk for awhile, building our writing community, and then move quietly back to our desks to write. I pull out my spiral, sit back in the rocking chair, and do the same. The students must see me modeling what I expect them to do. It deepens that sense of community, and they see the opportunities and values of writing are not only for them.

That first time the students may only write for about ten minutes. Watch and see how it is going because students' creativity and thinking can easily be stifled by closing too early, or they may experience discomfort with dragging the writing time out. As I see heads pop up, I ask the students to finish the thought they are on and come to a close. Next we share. (Fig. 4.1)

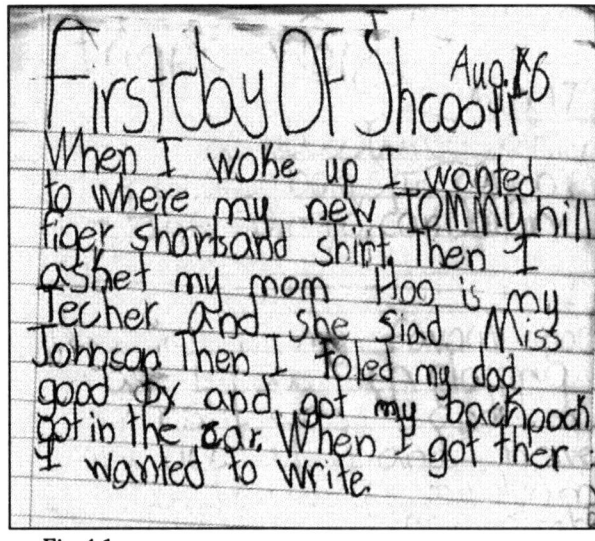
Fig. 4.1

Sharing

Talking about or reading what they write validates the words of the student. For a third grader, this is usually their favorite part. I devote at least fifteen minutes of this first day, more if needed because of its importance, to a student volunteering to read a sentence or a whole story. I do not force every child to read because I want students to feel they can take risks when they are ready.

After a few days, I introduce a concrete item they receive when they share. In the writing institute, when a participant shares a piece of writing, they may tie a knot in a rope or add a bead to a string. I modified these ideas. One day as I was cleaning out my drawers, I noticed all of the stickers I had collected. I had never used the stickers on graded papers because the students told me they got thrown away or torn off. I decided that every time students share their writing, they could place a sticker on their "Writing Tools" folders. I show the students where the stickers are kept, and just as I trust adults in the institute, I trust students to grab a sticker when they have earned it. As students conference and group share, they continue to add a sticker for each time they read their pieces.

Artifacts

An artifact in history is an object of archaeological or historical interest. In writing, it is the same. It is a concrete object that stands as a reminder to students of a book or a strategy we have learned. For example, in *Little Cliff's First Day of School*, Cliff wears a green corduroy hat given to him by his grandmother as a part of his new school clothes. I buy a piece of green corduroy and cut it in to small squares, one for each child. Even on the last day of school, the students can reach in to their artifact bag, pull out the green corduroy fabric, and summarize the story of both Cliff's and their own first day. I like students to have a special place to hold their artifacts all year. On days when they are stuck for an idea or strategy, they retrieve an artifact of a strategy that has worked for them before. They have a tangible item to trigger their memories. Ideas I have used in the past include a paper or plastic shoebox, a hand-sewn bag, or a store bought container. Those can get expensive and take up a lot of space. What I have found easiest and most practical is a simple white bag, either a paper sack or a gift bag I have purchased in mass quantity. Each student decorates his or her bag using markers, glitter, and paint. I have coat rack hooks to hang them on, or if those aren't available, I staple the bags to the wall.

Artifacts can be expensive if you do not plan ahead. My first couple of years, I went overboard out of enthusiasm and did not think about the best use of each object. Now, I try to have some type of artifact at least once a week, either for a new strategy we learn or for a special reading/writing connection. I use stickers, three dimensional objects, and sometimes photocopied pictures on small piece of paper. Places like Oriental Trading Company, U.S. Toys, and large variety chains sell larger quantities of items that you could purchase with another teacher. The joy on students' faces, triggered by literacy memories, as they pull out an artifact long forgotten, makes the extra effort of planning for these special objects a use of valuable time.

Recommended books for the first day of school.

Picture Books:
First Day Jitters by Julie Danneberg
First Year Letters by Julie Danneberg
First Day, Hooray! By Nancy Poydor
Incredible Me! by Kathi Appelt
The Brand New Kid by Katie Couric
Don't Laugh at Me by Steve Seskin and Allen Shamblin

Chapter Books:
Judy Moody by Megan McDonald
Back to School, Mallory by Laurie B. Friedman

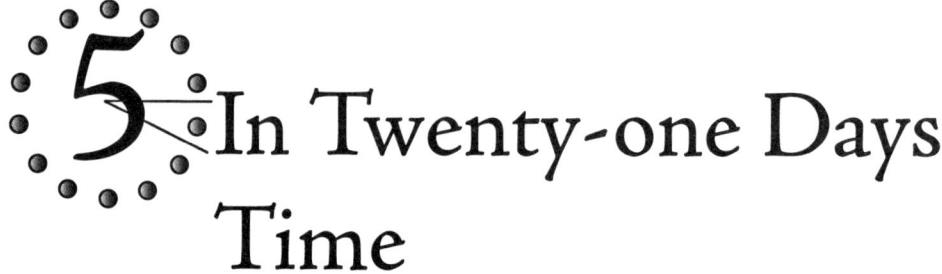 In Twenty-one Days Time

"Life offers two great gifts—time, and the ability to choose how we spend it. Planning is a process of choosing among those many options. If we do not choose to plan, then we choose to have others plan for us."
Richard I. Winword

When I left my three-week NJWPT/Abydos Writing Institute, I finished with so many new ideas and strategies, as well as an excitement about writing I had never felt before. Then I got scared. I was not sure how I was going to implement all of this in my classroom. What would I do first? When? How? Who would help me? Questions fluttered in and out of my mind.

After eight years in a third-grade classroom, I have learned that besides starting from day one, a writing teacher must provide a strong and steady base of lessons those first few weeks to prepare students for writing all year. I've always heard that a habit takes twenty-one days to develop. To me, the writing habit simply takes daily writing.

To provide those moments of daily writing that I call the Writing Workshop, I teach procedures and allow time for students to experience the writing process in a non-threatening way. In my overall schedule, Writing Workshop accounts for about an hour a day. These first few weeks allow for varying amounts of time in establishing a strong routine.

The following twenty-one days of lessons will help foster the habit of daily writing.

Day One
Lesson Focus: Reading / Writing Connection and Artifact Bags
Materials Needed: *Little Cliff's First Day of School* by Clifton L. Taulbert
                green corduroy
                white lunch sacks
                glitter
                markers, paint
Procedures: (See chapter 1—Time to Start)

Day Two

Lesson Focus: Trigger Words
Materials Needed: bag or basket
summer items such as sunscreen, beach towel
toy car
toy airplane
food item
baseball
and an object representing a TV or movie character
a book

Procedures: "The idea [of trigger words] is to jog a memory with a carefully chosen word" or in this case an object (Carroll & Wilson 67). Since the students are so excited about sharing what they did during the summer with me and everyone else, I wanted to put a twist on the traditional "What I Did On My Summer Vacation." Written on the board as the students come in that day is the Henry James quote, "Summer afternoon—Summer afternoon... the two most beautiful words in the English language." I use a beach sand pail as my basket to hold my items. I place at least five traditional and nontraditional summer items inside it. For example: a bottle of sunscreen, a toy airplane or car, a book, a box of band-aids, and a baseball. I don't tell the students anything about the items except to explain that we are using a prewriting strategy to help start our thinking. As I pull out each item, I ask the students to write the name of the object down so they are creating a list. If they have an immediate thought, they may jot that down alongside the item name. When I have pulled out the last item, I ask the students if any of the objects jogged a memory or made them immediately think of a story they want to tell.

We share those orally first. Then I ask them to start by choosing one item to write about, whatever it made them think of. If they want, they may write about more than one item or group a few together. That tends to happen naturally and sometimes unexpectedly for them. At first they may write simple sentences with maybe two lines about an object (Fig. 5.1). This allows for more expansion later as they become more familiar with the process and more comfortable with each other. After a designated time, usually about fifteen minutes, I ask a few volunteers to share. I tell them that tomorrow we will talk more about our objects.

On this day I also begin a prewriting anchor chart where we place the different strategies to help us prewrite as we experience them. We add the reading/writing connections from day one and trigger words from day two.

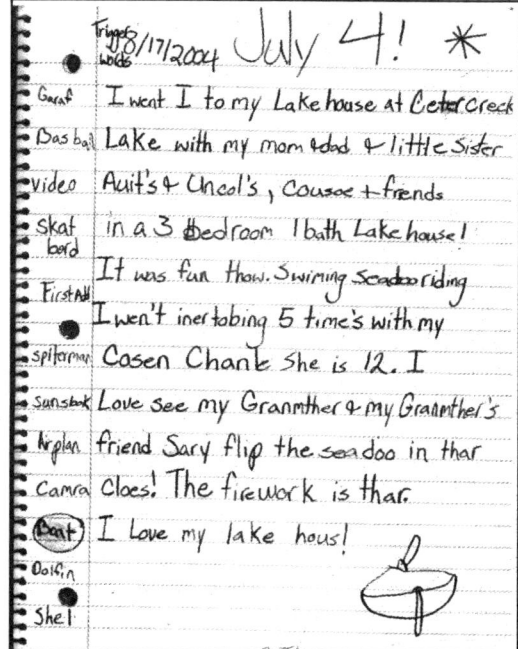

Fig. 5.1

Day Three

Lesson focus: Prewriting strategy—Brainstorming
Materials Needed: *How I Spent My Summer Vacation* by Mark Teague, seashells
Procedures: To continue our writing from day two, I ask the students if they thought that any of the objects had something in common. After awhile, and sometimes with prompting from me, we talk about the summer connection. It amazes them to look and see that many of them wrote about a summer experience without me ever assigning it. I read *What I Did on My Summer Vacation* by Mark Teague, and we talk about how each person's summer is different. I tell them that my summer basket would be filled with objects pertaining to the ocean and the beach and on an anchor chart titled "Summer" I begin to list items that remind me of summer, such as seashells, sand, cresting waves, Galveston, and so on. I then have them brainstorm a list of everything they can think of that reminds them of summer. After we share our lists, I ask them to draw a star by one or two of the items that they would most like to write about, and I give them time to do just that.

Many of their items follow a similar theme, as mine did, so I model how they could be grouped together. I also remind them that if they already started a story that they would like to continue working on, they may do that as well. As they begin writing they see me pull out my writer's notebook and write too. After a few minutes of modeling I walk around and conference with a few students, mainly concentrating on those having trouble getting started. This lesson is a precursor to our many future focus lessons. I started with a huge topic–summer–and asked them to narrow it down to one story or memory.

We always end the writing time by sharing what we wrote. It helps to build that trust and respect for each other's ideas.

We add "brainstorming" to our prewriting anchor chart. My artifact for them is a seashell that I have collected at the beach during the summer.

Possible extensions

Books about the beach that I read, exhibit or share are
The Seashore Book by Charlotte Zolotow for visualizing and description,
Hello Ocean by Pam Munoz Ryan to describe the five senses,
Beach is to Fun A Book About Relationships by Pat Brisson which explains analogies,
and *Have You Been To The Beach Lately?* a book of poems by Ralph Fletcher to introduce the genre of poetry.

Day Four

Lesson Focus: Writing about their names
Materials Needed: *The Name Quilt* by Phyllis Root

large index cards
Word Wizard by Cathryn Falwell

Procedures: The lessons I do using the student's names can take about a two-hour chunk on this day because I combine spelling, "getting to know you" activities, and writing. You can pick and choose what works or spread these ideas out over a few days. I begin by giving students a large index card upon which to write their name, and then they add a drawing of their face. This card will be used all year for graphing activities, but today we will use it for a working with words/spelling lesson. We place each card in a pocket chart, and the students begin to tell me how we could categorize the names. We begin to sort the cards, and I eventually steer the students toward grouping the names by syllables.

I read them *Word Wizard* by Cathryn Falwell and we talk about how we can rearrange letters in words to make new words. This familiarizes them with a spelling concept we will touch on all year, "making big words," from the Patricia M. Cunningham book, *Making Words*. Each child has letter boxes that already have multiple letters of the alphabet cut out and stored. If you don't have these letter boxes in your classroom, you may have to have the students print the letters of their names and cut them out. I use the letters in their first and last name so they have more letters to work with. On day three we just move the letters around and see what little words we can make using the letters in our names. For example, if I were doing my first name, Robin, I could move some letters around and pull them out to make the two-letter words *in*, *no*, and *or*, and the three-letter words *rob*, *rib* and *bin*. I model how I manipulate my letters and then walk around and help them do the same.

Later, we sit in a circle and play the "name game." I have the students use alliteration to tell about themselves. I start with "Robin likes to read." They may say something they like or don't like, "Sarah doesn't like snakes." Each person repeats the sentences they heard before them, with help from the class, and we learn names quickly and a little bit about each student. We use this activity to jumpstart our thinking for a name acrostic. I love how all of these activities flow together and help my students learn about each other.

As we move into another writing activity for the day, I read *The Name Quilt* by Phyllis Root. We talk about the uniqueness of

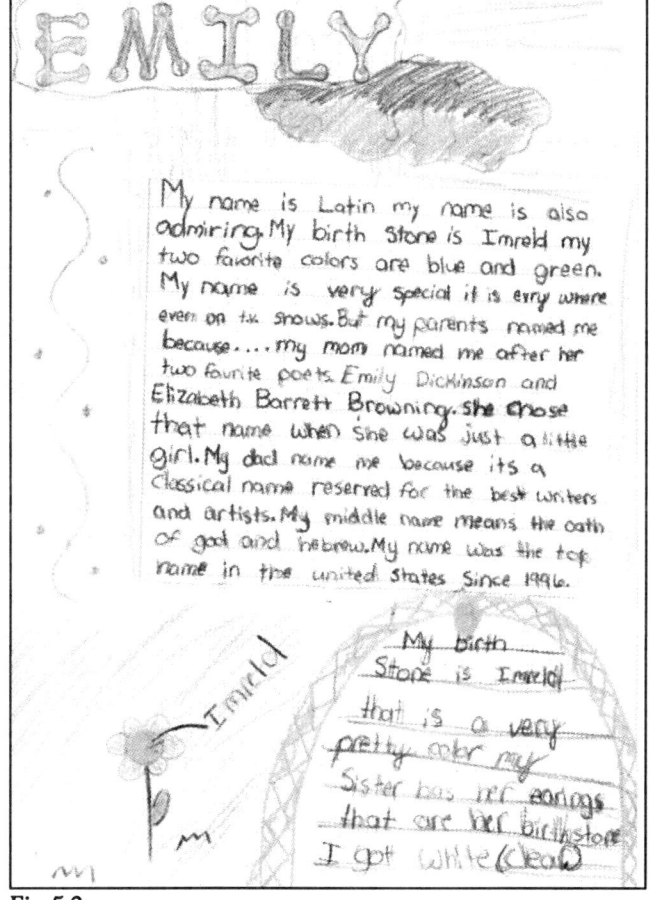
Fig. 5.2

our names and how we each have a story. I tell the students why my mother named me Robin and what I found out that Robin means. Some of the students already know their name's origin, but many don't. I ask them to talk to their parents about the origin of their names and be ready to share. We even look up some of names on the Internet to find out the meanings. Of course, it is natural for them to write about their names (Figs. 5.2., 5.3., 5.4). The next day we share our findings, and they have one more entry in their writing journals. Another book that is wonderful to encourage writing and sharing about names is *The First Thing My Mama Told Me* by Susan Marie Swanson.

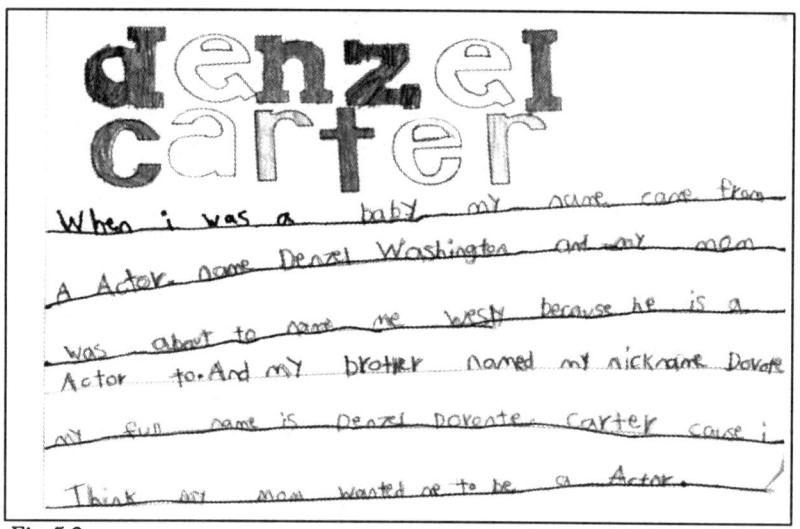

Fig. 5.3

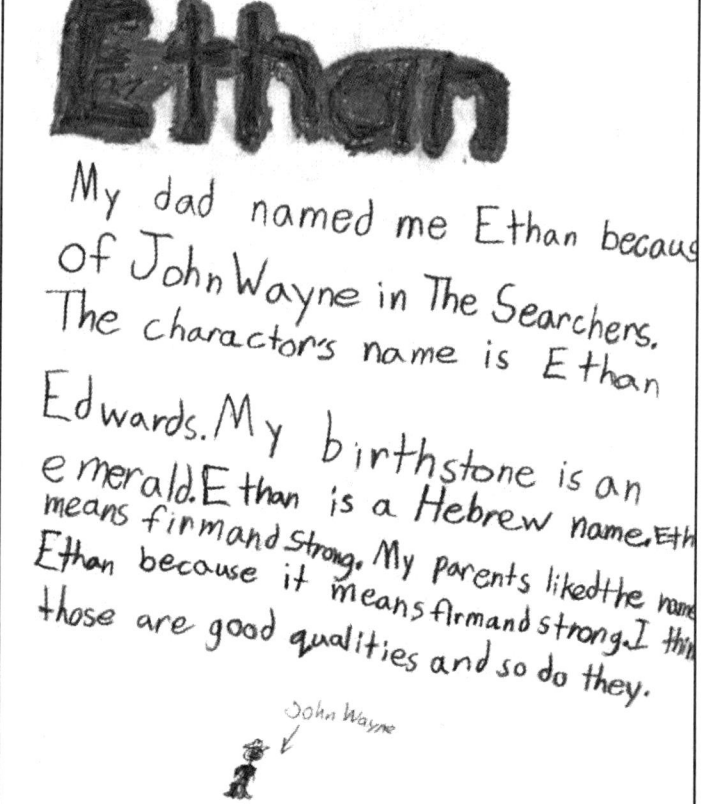

Fig. 5.4

Day Five

Lesson Focus: The "wonderful world of third grade"
Materials Needed: CD of the song, "What a Wonderful World" by Louis Armstrong
the book, *What a Wonderful World* by George David Weiss and Bob Thiele
index cards

Procedures: On the fifth day of school, I use the book titled and illustrated based on the words to the Louis Armstrong song, "What a Wonderful World." As the CD plays, I show the students the pictures from the book. We talk about being positive and how even if we have a bad day or week, we can find the "wonderful" in life. They have a choice to write today on paper or index cards. That fifth day they write about something wonderful that happened to them the first week of school. Each Friday after that as a way to end the school week and reflect, they write about any area of their life, school, sports, hobbies, or home.

Fig. 5.5

I have a bulletin board with the students' pictures (I have invited them to bring photos of themselves) and they place their written reflection next to their picture (Fig. 5.5). This is a special time when we come together and celebrate successes. I have never had a child who couldn't find at least one good moment during a week to write about. (If you have a child who has had major downfalls in a week, try to do something for them on Friday to brighten their day and maybe create that "wonderful" memory.) When we take down the writing from the bulletin board, we add it to our "Writing Tools" folder, and the students flip through these later for story ideas or as encouragement on a hard day. At the end of the year, we write something wonderful about each other and add it to our folder.

Day Six

Lesson Focus: What does writing look like?
Materials Needed: *Read Anything Good Lately?* by Susan Allen
chart paper
types of reading and writing that you do such as email, cookbook,
menu, instruction manual, book, and magazine

Procedures: The lesson on day six is about introducing students to text and genres of writing. I begin by making another anchor chart titled "Things we can read or write." Asking them what types of reading they do during the day allows them to think personally first, and they usually come up with the basics: chapter books, picture books, nonfiction, fiction, magazines, and maybe a few specific genres like mysteries. Then we look around the room to see what writing surrounds us, such as the cafeteria menu and the schedule.

Next, I pull out my book bag and show them what I have been reading in the last few

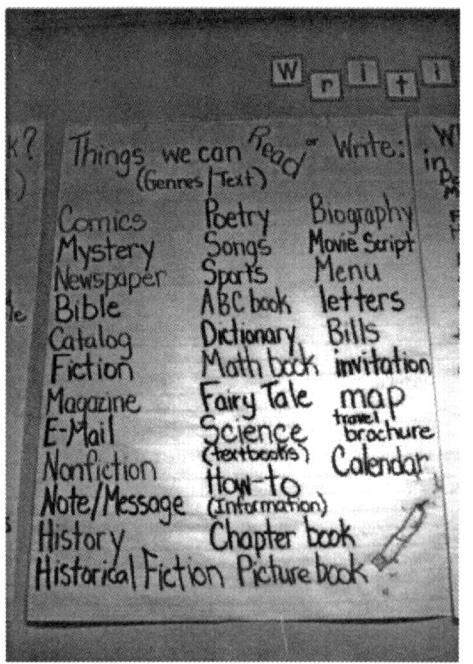

Fig. 5.6

days. I have an instruction manual for putting together my new TV, a cook book, an email about school, a letter from a friend, and, of course, a book I am reading. This really stirs their thinking.

They then begin to list these things and more. In the past I have made a tree trunk where they have written the genres on leaves, and we have added new leaves as we make new discoveries. I leave the chart on the wall all year so the students have an instant resource if they are stuck for a writing idea or if they want to try a new publishing format. I finish this lesson with the book *Read Anything Good Lately?* by Susan Allen, and as they share what they have read, we add even more genres to the anchor chart (Fig. 5.6). Finally, I give the students writing time to work on the writing they have already started in their notebooks or they can try one of these new ideas we have brainstormed. Then we share.

Day Seven

Lesson Focus: Purpose of our writer's notebook
Materials Needed: multiple copies of books with characters who keep a journal, such as the *Amelia's Notebook* series by Marisa Moss, *Harriet the Spy* by Louise Fitzhugh, and *Max's Logbook* by Marisa Moss, chart paper
Procedures: These first few weeks I want to saturate the students with topics and ideas that they can pull from and utilize all year during workshop time. Today's lesson is one more way to do that. On the desks I have spread out as many books as I can find of characters who keep journals or notebooks, such as the Amelia series. I let the students discover for themselves what kinds of writings the characters put in their journal.

Amelia uses her journal for her thoughts, her dreams, a list of friends, letters, directions, fictional stories, and so much more. As the students explore, they add all of these topics to an anchor chart fittingly entitled, "Things We Can Put in Our Writer's Notebook." This is where I make the point of letting students know that their writer's notebook is special and completely theirs. I may ask them at times to include some of the class lesson in there, but they are free to take it with them wherever they go and write in it as soon as a thought hits them. To keep the writing momentum flowing, we continue working on pieces already started, or we try something new from a minilesson. As always, we end with sharing. (Fig. 5.6)

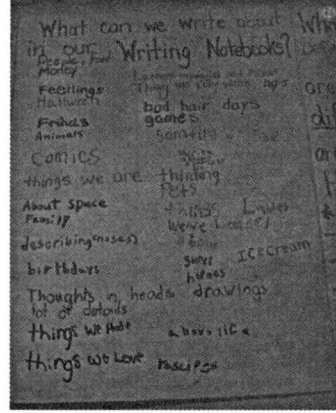

Fig. 5.6

Day Eight

Lesson Focus: Writing is a recursive process, making a "snake"
Materials Needed: *You Have To Write* by Janet Wong
white paper
chart paper
a slinky(ies)

Fig. 5.7

Procedures: After I had been through my three-week institute, another teacher showed me a new strategy she had learned in hers—a hands-on way to introduce the recursiveness of the writing process developed by Carol Wishheimer.

Many of my third graders don't have any knowledge of the stages of the process except prewriting because that is usually their main focus. Or they have had teachers who walked them through each stage, and they misunderstood the process to be linear.

I read *You Have to Write* by Janet Wong. Then I show them a slinky; and, if I can afford it, I buy them each a small one as well. We play with the slinky and watch how it folds into itself and rocks back and forth. I connect this to writing. We talk about all of the writing we have been doing and how we may have lots of pieces started, but we have not yet finished anything completely. On the board I draw a coil that looks a lot like the slinky folded down flat. We divide the coil into quadrants and choose a different color for each quadrant. One quadrant is labeled prewriting, one drafting, one revising/editing, and one publishing. I tell the students these are the stages their writing will go through and all year we will learn new strategies and understand the depths of each stage. For now, our focus is to realize writers move in and out of each stage as they write.

The students cut the coil and see that it approximates the slinky. I show them a piece of my writing from the beginning to the end, how it has entered many drafts, has mark outs, messiness, and how it changes to its eventual order. They now have visuals through a concrete object (slinky), a graphic form (coil), and an actual piece of writing to see how the process works (Fig. 5.7). We go back through our notebook and look at what parts of the process we have already experienced. We make sure we have been keeping up with our prewriting chart, and then we write and share.

Day Nine

Lesson Focus: Things I Can Write About and Writing Tools Folder
Materials Needed: *Judy and the Volcano* by Wayne Harris

notebook paper
students' folders bound and ready to be put together

Procedures: I want students to see the value of gathering thoughts and ideas for their year long/life long writing so we continue a few more days of prewriting. This helps them feel comfortable with short bursts of writing and builds confidence in sharing. They realize they have lots to write about and there is interest in what they have to say. There are commonalities and they develop a community from their writing. On day nine, I read *Judy and the Volcano* by Wayne Harris and stop on the page where she says she can't think of anything to write. I make a big deal about how even a made-up character gets stuck; it happens to us all, and we infer that it must have happened to the author. We divide a piece of notebook paper up into quadrants and write: "People We Know" in one, "Places We've Been" in another, "Feelings We Have" in the third, and "Other Special Ideas" in the last one. Then the kids list underneath each. We work on this together and listen and learn from each other. This out-loud brainstorming sparks thoughts and ideas that are sometimes hidden. This is also the day we make sure we have put together our "Writing Tools" folder and labeled everything. We add our "Topics to Write About" sheet to its proper section so they are ready to write.

Day Ten
Lesson Focus: Prewriting strategy—Listing
Materials Needed: *1,400 Things for Kids to be Happy About* by Barbara Ann Kipfer
chart paper

Procedures: To coincide with our "Wonderful World" Fridays, we read *1,400 Things for Kids to be Happy About* by Barbara Ann Kipfer. I show them my adult version by the same author and tell them that I have had it since college ,and I pull it out for a giggle every now and then. I also tell them that as I read through the list, stories of those times that made me happy come to mind quickly, and I have to get them written down. Then we list things that make us happy, from the general to the specific. Afterwords, we choose one topic that pops out at us, and we begin to write. If you are thinking that the students are confused because they have started so many stories and not necessarily finished them, don't worry. Some days they are only writing two or three sentences. So the more of this prewriting that we do, the better a chance that a story that truly interests them will be brought to mind. Some already begin to see that the many stories they have started have themes running through them, like family or friendship, and they may combine two or more started pieces into one.

Day Eleven
Lesson Focus: Reading/Writing Connection and Grouping Strategy—Pointing
Materials Needed: *Emily's Art* by Peter Catalanotto
chart paper
5 sets of 4 different colored crayons (4 greens, 4 reds, etc.)

Procedures: We have many pieces started and we have been sharing whole class for a while now to build that feeling of a community of writers. By day eleven, I want them to commit to one of the pieces they like because we are going to do our first small group sharing strategy.

I place a crayon on each student's desk. I teach them the strategy of pointing (Carroll & Wilson 151). Today is all about feeling that our writing has worth and that others like what we write. We only point out something from the sharing that we like or think is interesting. The students usually come back from this small group share time feeling validated and ready to write more.

I end writing time with *Emily's Art* by Peter Catalannotto. I know that in the next few days we are going to be doing some drawing ourselves, so I want the students to hear about a character who takes a risk with her art. I want them to see how important it is not to judge each others work but to embrace it. They keep their crayon as an artifact.

Day Twelve

Lesson Focus: Prewriting strategy—Drawing (See Carroll's "Drawing into Meaning" in Carroll and Wilson)
Materials Needed: *All the Places To Love* by Patricia MacLachlan
watercolors
Procedures: Today, besides being about prewriting and drawing, begins our many future lessons on descriptive writing. The book *All the Places to Love* by Patricia MacLachlan has multiple functions. I choose to use it for this lesson because of the vibrant pictures and use of descriptive language. As I read, we discuss the way the author describes the special places and shows them through the illustrations. After I finish, the students sketch in their journal their favorite place or a place they love to go. I show them my sketch of the beach (Fig. 5.8). Then they actually turn their sketches into water-colored renditions. I buy a few watercolors for the students to share, and we talk extensively about keeping things clean and being careful with the supplies. This is all of the time we usually have for day twelve, so we let the pictures dry overnight and continue the next day.

Fig. 5.8

Fig. 5.9

Day Thirteen

Lesson Focus: Continue drawing part of prewriting
Materials Needed: *All the Places To Love* by Patricia MacLachlan
                      watercolors

Procedures: We go back to the story and revisit some of the descriptive language they heard from the author yesterday. I model writing about my favorite place, the beach (Figure 5.9). They then write about their favorite place and try to add their own descriptive flair. Eventually we will take these short descriptions through the process, type them up, add them to our watercolor picture, and display them for everyone to admire (Figs. 5.10, 5.11, 5.12, 5.13).

> The Place I Love Most
> When I'm playing baseball. Sometimes it feels good to have light soft dirt in your cleats. And to slide and not get in trouble. And to get dirty and not to get hurt . I Love baseball. Sometimes it smells really bad. And it will feel 95 degrees in pants. It is hot but the team has fun anyway. It tastes nasty when you get that dirt in your mouth when you slide. So the baseball field is my favorite place.
>   by Brandon Pelkey

Fig. 5.10

Fig. 5.11

> The Place I Love Most
> I could hear the seagulls, smell the air, feel the sand. The tide had hit the shore soothingly calm. After that we saw alot of fireworks with colors like purple, blue,yellow,red,orange,ect.
> We had a BIG beach party with the family. We had hotdogs, chips. After we all went to bed I was still awake thinking about the next day in Galveston, my favorite place.
>   by Brady Wilbanks.

Fig. 5.12

Fig. 5.13

Day Fourteen

Lesson Focus: Me Bag
Materials Needed: *Judy Moody* by Megan McDonald
                       paper sacks
                       index cards

Procedures: On the first day of school I begin reading *Judy Moody* by Megan McDonald during the reading time. The story focuses on a character who does not want to go to third grade and all of the things, good and bad, that happen to her in her first few weeks of school. This is my first read-aloud chapter book.

    The main character, Judy, has an assignment to make a "Me Collage" for school. We make a "Me Bag." I give the students paper sacks and on index cards they write a different object or picture from their life that truly represents them. They write a quick memory, story, or description about that object, why it is important, or how it symbolizes them. They may take the bag home and fill it with those items or pictures to bring back and share with the class. These index cards are kept in the sack and placed in their Writing Tools Folder so that at a later date we can go back and expand on each topic. For example, several students always bring a trophy they have won playing a sport. They now have the beginning of a story about the time they won that trophy. They may choose to begin writing that story today or come back to it when they want to start something new on a different day.

Day Fifteen

Lesson Focus: Prewriting—Webbing
Materials Needed: *Dear Mrs. LaRue* by Mark Teague
                       dog biscuits

Procedures: Today I am ready to start working through each stage of the process with the students. It will be a quick overview, but it will allow those who are ready to use their workshop time to move forward and go into more depth with their pieces. Every time I read *Dear Mrs. LaRue* by Mark Teague it reminds me of when my dog, Hershey, was a puppy and got in so much trouble that some days I thought I would send him off to obedience school. Because I have so many connections to the book, I know I have plenty to write. Pets can be one of those topics that is huge and overwhelming, so I chose a web as a way to organize my ideas. I let the students ask me questions about Hershey so that they can see how the questions prompt my thinking and inspire me to add more to the spokes of my

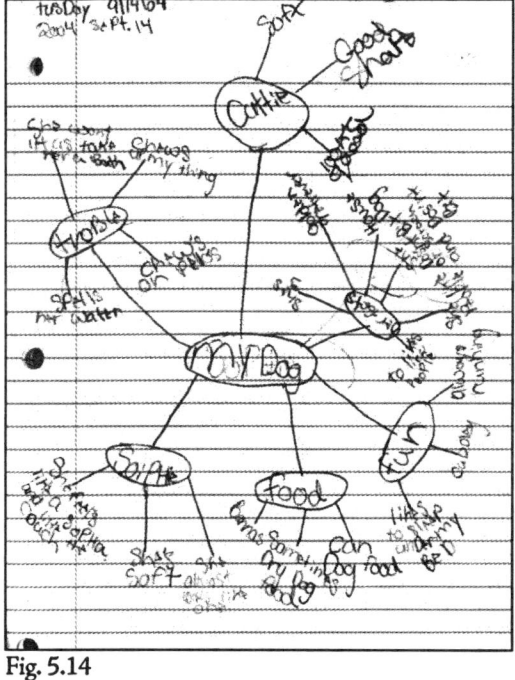

Fig. 5.14

web (Fig. 5.13). They then choose a topic of interest. Many choose their pet, but some choose a friend, a sport, or a hobby.

They spend the rest of their writing time today creating their web. I use a dog biscuit (about $2.19 per hundred) as an artifact for this lesson. Another book about pets I like to introduce is *My Big Dog* by Susan Stevens Crummel and Janet Stevens because it is about a friendship between a cat and a dog.

Day Sixteen
Lesson Focus: Introduce Drafting Stage, Status of the Class
Materials Needed: *What Do Author's Do* by Eileen Christelow
        chart paper
        overhead and transparency

Procedures: I begin today's lesson with Nanci Atwell's "Status of the Class" (Atwell, 1998, 107). As each child tells me what their web was about yesterday, I write it down. If I write it on my teacher notes then I have a record of the topic they are working on and a good idea where they stand. Sometimes I will write the topics on a chart so everyone can see the topics started. If they get stuck later, they can refer back to the chart and hopefully come up with a topic for themselves. I pull out my web from day fifteen about Hershey and talk about how I work as a writer.

I model how I transfer the information from my web into a story. I model my thinking out loud as I write. I skip lines, mark a line through a word instead of erasing, and use only one side of the paper. I do this out of habit, but I tell the students that later they will see why those drafting tips help me through the process. I tell them not to worry about perfect papers, just to get their thoughts down in some kind of form. They may use black ballpoint during writing time because I find that this makes it harder for them to erase. They go back to their desks and begin to draft.

Day Seventeen
Lesson Focus: Introduce Revising Stage and model an example
Materials Needed: *What Do Author's Do* by Eileen Christelow
        chart paper
        overhead and transparency

Procedures: I know that for some students it takes a lot longer than one day to draft a story. These lessons are not about finishing each stage of the process. They are about allowing the students to engage in each part of the process and experience the basics. I remind them that we will work through the pieces of each stage all year as they write. Each day from this point in the process until we get to publishing, I read a few pages of *What Do Author's Do* by Eileen Christelow. This gives them an overview of the stages an author goes through. Today I pull out my transparency or chart where I drafted my story yesterday about Hershey. I point out that I was already revising as I wrote. I show them the places that I marked out and changed words, where I rearranged sentences, or have added something. I reread my story to see if there is anything else I want to change or add. I invite them do the same to their story.

One way that I encourage revising is to permit the students to use a different colored pen or gel pen to make their changes. It adds a little excitement and creates a visual cue for going back and reentering their writing. I allow them time to continue drafting and revising so that they are ready for another grouping strategy tomorrow. I spend most of my time today monitoring and conferencing so that I can help scaffold students as they move deeper into their writing.

Day Eighteen

Lesson Focus: Continue drafting and revising, grouping strategy—Say Back
Materials Needed: None
Procedures: Today I have the students number off from one to four to get into their small share groups. Say Back is a great grouping strategy for this stage of the process because it suggests more ways to revise for those students who think they are finished (Carroll & Wilson 157). Besides sharing something positive as they did with "Pointing," they now ask a question about a part of the story they want to know more about. I model first with a student who volunteers to read his or her writing, and I use my story that I started about Hershey. Usually they ask me about how big he is or when he was born or something I have intentionally left out. I have them write their say back responses on a post-it®, and they place it on the spot in my draft where it belongs (Fig. 5.15).

I then show them how I go back into my story and add that information to make it more complete. It also shows them why I skip lines—to leave space for changes. They then go to their groups, share, come back and revise in the places where they want to add information.

Fig. 5.15

Day Nineteen

Lesson Focus: Introduce Editing stage and model an example
Materials Needed: *What Do Author's Do* by Eileen Christelow
                chart paper
                overhead and transparency
Procedures: Today we move to the editing stage. All year we will work on different parts of editing, but today I am going to focus on one or two skills that I know they have seen before in lower grades. We use a Word Wall for our high frequency spelling words. I have purposely misspelled one of our Word Wall words in my draft so that I can model going back and editing. I use a different color once again and show them how I find a misspelled word and change it: I circle a word if I think it looks wrong but am not sure what is right. Then I will have a reminder that I need to look that word up later.

I can also check to make sure I have capitalized my title and any names I have used in the story. Today I may only have my students look for those same things too. I don't want them to be overwhelmed at this point, just to understand what editing is in a piece. In *What Do Author's Do* by Eileen Christelow, we learn about sending a piece off to an editor, and they see the importance of this stage.

Day Twenty

Lesson Focus: What is publishing?
Materials Needed: *What Do Author's Do* by Eileen Christelow
    chart paper
    overhead and transparency

Procedures: Today we talk about how we could finish our piece. We go back to the chart we made about all the different types of writing. We think about typing up our story or rewriting it neatly. If we wanted to add pictures, where could they go? We pull out children's books that we are reading and see how the publishing looks in those books. We want our final pieces to look as if they were ready to be sold in a third-grade store. Most of the students are not to this point yet, so they continue writing, and I continue conferencing.

Day Twenty-One

Lesson Focus: Writing Workshop begins, status of the class, and teacher conferencing
Materials Needed: chart paper

Procedures: By this time students are working in all the different stages of the process. Conferencing with the students helps keep up with who is working on what. Today, some are still drafting. Others want help with their editing. A few may be ready to conference about how they are going to publish this first story. It is an exciting time, letting them move at their own pace and finish their first published piece.

6 The Rest of the Time

"The best thing about the future is that it comes one day at a time".
Abraham Lincoln

You might be thinking, "Great, I have twenty-one days of lessons, but what about the next 160 days?" The first few lessons are only a starting point to your daily workshop time. The following pages provide additional lessons that can be plugged into your existing framework.

Prewriting Lessons

Blueprinting

In *Acts of Teaching*, Carroll and Wilson state that blueprinting "allows students to re-create places that hold memories that they then may choose to write about" (73). I begin, as I do with most lessons, by reading a picture book. There are several that work well with the idea of blueprinting, but my favorite is *Let's Go Home: The Wonderful Things About a House* by Cynthia Rylant. I only read a few pages at first to encourage thinking about a house. At this point in the year, we have already done our lesson on their favorite place. Consequently, the students have written about baseball fields, restaurants, and outdoor arenas. I focus this blueprinting lesson on an inside place, house, apartment, or building.

First the students need to understand what a *blueprint* entails. I bring in the actual blueprints for my house. I tell them that my husband and I bought this house eight years ago, our first together as a couple. I sketch out a blueprint on paper to model what they will do next. As I sketch I share why we liked the house and a few things about each room that make them special. I label each room as I draw it. Over to the side, I begin to list the rooms, leaving space between each one.

Then I write—memories, feelings, or snippets of events that happened in that particular room. I show the students how to let the ideas flow and not get caught up on sentences or thinking too much. We write what we remember or what we see in our minds as we picture that room. The visual of the blueprint sparks images from those rooms that the students might not have thought about in a while.

After a few moments spent focusing on each room, I model choosing the memory or anecdote that I want to write more about. We all spend about fifteen minutes writing. After we share, the students have a wealth of prewriting they can return to at another time, and I read the rest of *Let's Go Home*. Other books I have used are: *Homeplace* by Crescent Dragonwagon and *Our Old House* by Susan Vizurrago.

Blueprinting became an even more memorable writing event for me when I used a new book of poems I bought titled *Home to Me: Poems Across America* by Lee Bennett Hopkins. The poems in the book deal with all types of homes, including trailers, mansions, tents, and apartment buildings. I chose to use this book with the students in my school in mind, including one who had been displaced by Hurricane Katrina. That student often wrote disjointed stories of his time in New Orleans, so I wanted him to focus on the memories of his house or a special place for him that he missed. He shared for the first time about his life back in Louisiana and promised me he would continue writing to keep his memories alive.

A Writer's Eyes

At the beginning and then once again toward the middle of the year, when my students feel as if they are running out of writing topics, I teach this lesson. I read *Nothing Ever Happens on 90th Street* by Roni Schotter. The character must write something, anything as an assignment for her teacher due the next day. She is stuck, so she sits on her front porch step and watches what is happening on her street, which is quite a lot. She sees her surroundings and the everyday occurrences in a new light, one that she writes down.

I give my students a ring to wear with movable eyeballs on it, or for less money, I buy a set of wiggly eyes they can attach to their writing spirals. We spread out around our school building and sit and watch the people who walk by. My students take notes on what is happening in front of them. When we share back in the classroom, we discuss how each of us noticed different things and people. Some areas of the building had really interesting events going on and some places were quiet. I tell the students that everything around us can become a story if we use our "writer's eyes." We can turn an ordinary event into an extraordinary story. We try it with something they saw, such as the kids who were putting up their lunch trays in the cafeteria.

One student created a fantasy lunch menu; one wrote about a boy with super powers who changes the lunch rules; and another student wrote about how nervous she was on her first day in the "big kid" lunchroom. They wrote multiple genres and from multiple points of view. I encourage the students to keep their writer's eyes on at home and when they travel. Many students take their writing spirals home daily to capture the things they see and want to write about at another time.

Looping

Focusing on a topic and narrowing it down is one of the things my students struggle with most. With Looping, students write a topic at the top of their page. It can be a subject they are studying in a content area or a big idea like friendship. After a few minutes of writing on that topic, the students read what they have written and look for that word or phrase that grabs their attention, one they want to elaborate on or add more to. That "center of gravity" becomes the new idea that they write about on their second loop (Carroll & Wilson 74). They do this once or twice more depending on what else they have to say.

Some students find an idea repeated over and over so that becomes their new focused topic. Others have created paragraphs detailing their original topic. I use this activity to assess students' knowledge of a subject area, such as states of matter in science or a history lesson. Students who have trouble being too general or broad with a topic, such as "My Vacation" or "Thanksgiving" can use this approach to concentrate on the ideas that hold their attention and seem the most important.

Quicklist

Paula Brock, a fellow writing project trainer, in her book *Nudges* added a new dimension to making idea lists with the quicklist (5). Her original idea centered around making a list of important people in life, such as family and friends. Her first column contained names. The second column contained adjectives or descriptions of the person from column one. The last column became a place for anecdotes and short phrases about the person, memories triggered when the person's name was written.

Over the years I have read The *Relatives Came* by Cynthia Rylant or *When Lightening Comes in a Jar* by Patricia Polacco. Both books tell the importance of family stories and writing family history down for future generations. *The Name Quilt* by Phyllis Root, which I read at the beginning of the year, is a story that lends itself to family quicklists by showing the names of family members written on a special quilt, and then having the main character tell a funny or amazing story about the name. I first use the names and anecdotes from *The Name Quilt* to model a quicklist, and then I model a quicklist of my own family and friends.

I expanded my lesson on quicklists by having the students generate a list of people or occupations they felt were heroes. We read the book *Heroes* by Ken Mochizuki. I try to encourage them to think out of the box about the meaning of hero. I have a bucket of books about scientists, rescue workers, and ordinary people doing extraordinary things. As always, the students surprise me with the depth of their thinking, coming up with occupations such as lifeguards and animal shelter workers, as well as animals, such as dolphins who have been heroic.

To help with the descriptions and anecdotes, we choose quotes from the book about heroes, such as "He was a war hero," "Real heroes don't brag," and "They just do what they are supposed to do." Another character stated, "Heroes don't panic." We discussed synonyms for bravery and courage, then talk about how sometimes a hero doesn't feel brave, but does what is right because he or she knows it is best.

The quicklist opens the door to a new way of thinking about what might seem like a familiar topic. One of my students who loved cars decided to make a quicklist of cars he had read about and then wrote his own nonfiction book. I have seen students use the quicklist as their main strategy for finding ideas (Fig. 6.1).

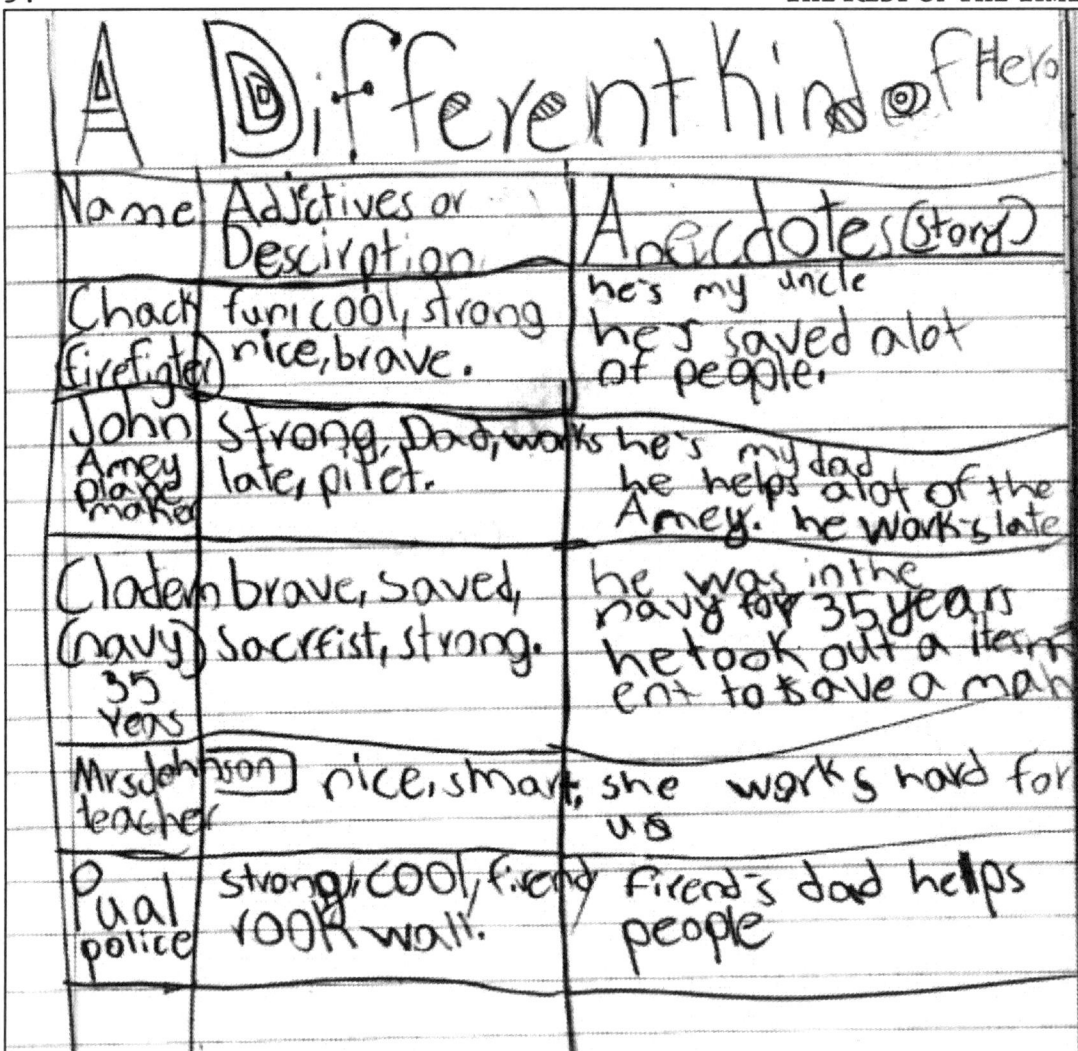

Fig. 6.1

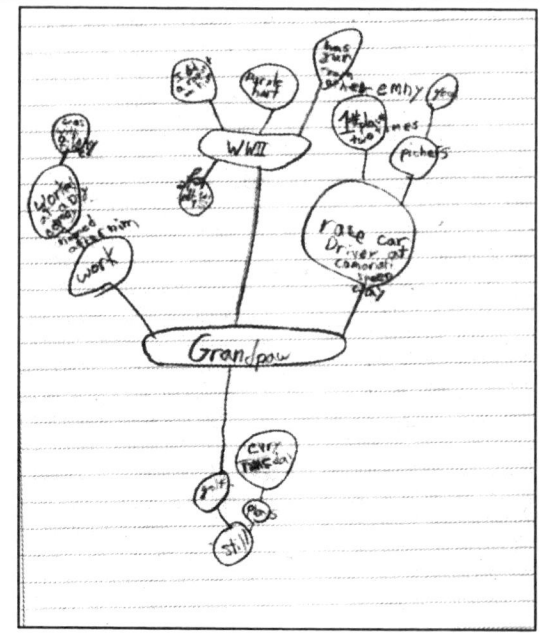

Fig. 6.2

Here is a student using his quick list, which he turns it into a web (Fig. 6.2). Notice in the quicklist, the student lists a variety of people, but the web allows the student to focus on one in particular. This process allows for students to develop depth.

Webbing a Story

Many students are introduced to the concept of webbing early in school. What I have noticed about much of the writing I see is that the web does not match what the students actually wrote. Somewhere they missed the part where they take their parts of the web and turn them into sentences. I model with a few paragraphs about one subject.

For example, during our study of celebrations, we read about piñatas. I place the word piñata on the middle of the page, the center of my web. The students and I must use the author's words from the paragraphs to create the legs of the web. Then, the students write their own paragraph about a piñata using the web and its ideas. I see for the first time a light in my students' eyes as they understood now how to go from web to draft. It is a step of learning some had never taken before in the writing process. Modeling, as always, is the key.

Around Thanksgiving, I use the book *I Know An Old Lady Who Swallowed A Pie* by Alison Jackson to make a web and transfer the details to our writing. Thanksgiving is one of those gigantic topics that students have trouble filtering down. The book focuses on the feast aspect of Thanksgiving, so we use the author's details of the feast to make a web. I show the students how one small part of the Thanksgiving holiday can be made into a whole story. We web other ideas surrounding this holiday—family, traveling, football games, and shopping. The students now have a better start to whittling down a broad topic into smaller chunks.

Drafting / Revising Lessons

Depth Charging

Joyce Armstrong Carroll shares a revising strategy known as "depth charging" in her book, *Dr. JAC's Guide To Writing With Depth* (5). This strategy works wonders for helping students vertically elaborate and add more specific details. To model depth charging, I begin with the books *Zoom* and *ReZoom* by Istvan Banyai. These books contain pictures that zoom in on specific parts of a big picture. The students find the focus of the picture and watch how adjusting that focus leads to more detail in *Zoom* and a bigger picture in *ReZoom*. I model this lesson many times throughout the year when I see students needing an extra push to show more detail. After sharing the books, I pull out a sentence from a story I composed with the class.

For example, I once shared about our hot water heater breaking over the weekend. I wrote, "On Sunday when we arrived home, our hot water heater had flooded the garage. It was a mess, but not as bad as it could have been." I reentered my paragraph and circled *garage* because I knew I could tell more about that word or phrase. I added, "Luckily, we had cleaned out the garage last summer so nothing was ruined". I also use this technique when we come back from a long weekend or holiday and the students tend to list what they did. When I write about our Thanksgiving turkey, I make my sentences short and simple. I can easily go back in and circle words to help me add depth, for example with *turkey*, or *house*. Circling a word to tell more about helps students focus in on one idea instead of the whole sentence or story. It breaks it down for them and gives them a concrete way to revise. For an artifact, I order small binoculars so students concretely practice zooming in on their own sentences.

Leads and Conclusions

My students have a hard time creating a lead sentence for their piece of writing. I model this concept with lots of children's books and lots of practice. We pull books out of our bucket and see how the author started the story. Usually the leads we see fall into the categories of action, setting, conversation, or a startling statement. We use a story we have started and see if we can try new leads with it. I model my own and then they write and share. I give the students a cut out fish or a plastic hook and talk about how fishermen have to choose a different hook or bait to reel in the fish they want. Writers are doing the same. The more the students try new ways to open stories, the better they become at choosing the most interesting way to "hook" the reader.

Another hard concept for my students is knowing when the story ends. The best way I have found to show the importance of concluding a story is by using Jodi Ramos' idea in *Elementary Minilessons* (19). I find pictures of animals that I put on a transparency. I white out their tails and ask the students what is wrong with the pictures. They immediately see their "ends" are missing. I then draw the wrong tails on each animal, a curly cue pig tail for the dog and a long bushy lion's tail for the horse. I tell the students that I corrected the problem; now they all have tail ends. They let me know right away that the tails don't match. Eyes open up! We connect this lesson immediately to our writing. Sometimes we forget the tails of our stories or we attach a tail that doesn't fit. Once again, consistent conclusions take the use of children's book examples, teacher modeling, and practice within the students' own writing. Many more ideas for writing conclusions come from Dr. Joyce Armstrong Carroll's book *Conclusions*.

Onomatopoeia

I teach onomatopoeia at the same time as I teach leads. My students like to use onomatopoeia or an action sequence to start a story. One of my favorite books is *Gerald McBoing Boing* by Dr. Seuss. The little boy speaks only in sounds. After I read this aloud, we list all of the onomatopoeic words the author used. We search through other books we have been reading and find more to add to our list. We have another ongoing resource to add to our word bank in our Writing Tools folder. During writing workshop on the day of this lesson, I will invite students to try to add one or two onomatopoeic words to a piece they are working on. At the end, we share what we added.

Revising/Editing Lessons

Words That Set the Mood

One of the lessons I do that lends itself well to any prompt about feelings, such as "A Time I was Afraid," is setting the tone. I read *The Graves Family* by Patricia Polacco. From the characters' names, Shalleaux and Doug Graves, to the crimson colors and murderous adjectives, this book shows how an author can make a story seem spooky through simple word choice. As we read, we listen for words that set the tone and list them on an anchor chart called "Words with a Fear Factor." If the students have chosen to write their own scary story, then they now have a word bank. We share other ways to set the tone for a story, such as using similes and metaphors and details. It is important during these lessons that I don't just limit my students to using the one mood we practiced, but help them see how words can set the feeling of any piece.

Fabulous Adjectives

Most students by third grade understand the concept of an adjective and can add one when you tell them to. *The Boy Who Cried Fabulous* by Leslea Newman takes the concept of overusing adjectives and turns it into a learning tool for how adjectives can add to your vocabulary in speech and writing. The main character describes everything he sees as *fabulous*. His parents ban the word, so by the end of the story he must find other words to describe what he sees, such as *magnificent, charming, wonderful*, and *stupendous*. We add these words to our word bank and practice enhancing our writing with them too.

This lesson leads into lessons on synonyms for overused words such as *said*. "Said is Dead" is a lesson that a writing trainer once taught me where the students make a tombstone for *said* and bury it. The obituary lists other words we can use in our writing instead of *said* now that it is gone.

Quotation Marks

Along with the "Said is Dead" synonym lesson, I talk about using speaking and quotation marks within stories correctly. I read *What! Cried Granny: An Almost Bedtime Story* by Kate Lum where the grandmother and the grandson have a funny and exasperating conversation back and forth throughout the book. I rewrite some of their quotes and sentences up on the board. The author repeats many of the same words, such as *cried* and *said*. We talk about why we think she did that and we look at how we could change some of those words to other words that would convey the same tone, such as *shouted* or *replied*. This discussion leads us into the lesson on using quotation marks.

I talk about how my grandmother always had words of wisdom for me, like "You can do anything you want if you work hard" or the nickname she gave me from birth, "Robin bird." I ask them if they can tell me things that their parents repeat, words of wisdom, commands, or daily sayings. If the students are stuck, I read a little from *My Momma Likes To Say* and *My Teacher Likes To Say* both by Denise Brennan-Nelson.

We use two paper plates held together by a brad. On the top plate, we draw a mouth and cut it out. Then, on the bottom plate we write the sayings that we want to use as examples, either ones we think of from home or school. To cement the idea of using quotation marks when someone is speaking in a story, I give the students lip stickers to place around the mouth where the sayings will be written. The students can decorate the top plate to look like whomever is speaking, and, because of the brad, the plates will rotate so more than one saying can be seen. We keep these quotation people in our Writing Tools folder so that when we want to have characters speaking in our writing, we can remember to indent and to make sure the quotation marks are there along with interesting "said" words.

Punctuation

Punctuation Takes a Vacation by Robin Pulver teaches kids the effectiveness of using punctuation marks correctly. The punctuation marks leave and go on vacation. We take the part where the punctuation marks send postcards describing what they are doing back to the classroom and use the author's model to make our own punctuation postcards as a concrete reminder of the importance of punctuation for the writer to convey meaning and for the reader to understand that meaning.

Expanding Vocabulary and Synonyms

In *Words, Words, Words,* Janet Allen writes, "Making vocabulary study meaningful and useful for students has always been the difficult part. As teachers we must help students incorporate new words into their existing language in ways that don't seem phony" (40).

Miss Alaineus: A Vocabulary Disaster by Debra Frasier is about a girl who misses the spelling list on Monday because she is sick, and when her friend reads the list over the phone, she misinterprets *miscellaneous* to be a woman. This book encourages the kids who struggle with spelling and understanding vocabulary.

Thesaurus Rex by Laya Steinberg is a fun reminder to the kids that there are different ways to say and write words we use in our everyday language.

Donovan's Word Jar by Monalisa DeGross is a book that I like to use at the beginning of the year so that we can have a word jar in our class in which we collect interesting words we find all year in books, newspapers, and each other's writing.

Spelling

In *The War Between the Vowels and the Consonants*, Priscilla Turner reminds us how all of the alphabet must work together to form words and be understood. As I read this to kids, they easily see the implications of how spelling and putting letters together must happen in their writing so that the sentences make sense and create coherence.

Ratiocination

Ratiocination is a word that becomes a favorite of my kids to say, not only because it sounds made up, but because it is a concrete strategy they love to use to revise and edit their papers. Joyce Armstrong Carroll, in *Acts of Teaching,* writes that ratiocination "invites the students, through a process of coding and decoding clues, to manipulate sentences, consider syntax and diction, activate verbs, vary sentence beginnings, avoid weak repetition, refresh clichés, and in general develop and clarify their thinking and writing" (226).

My students and I love mysteries, so when I model ratiocination, I give them a small magnifying glass as an artifact and tell them they are becoming writing detectives who search for clues. We have a concrete code for each part of their writing and a clue for what I want them to search for and recognize. I always start by inviting the students to choose two different crayons. They underline their writing in one color until they come to their first ending punctuation mark, a period, question mark, or exclamation point. Then they switch colors and do the same with the next sentence. Marking the sentences in this way originally taught students to vary their sentence length. Some of my students understand that more toward the end of the year, but in the beginning, it is a powerful tool for showing a lack of punctuation.

Many of my students come away with only one color underlining everything. They immediately recognize the fact that they did not use an end mark. It provides a perfect opportunity for me to do a reteach with those students on complete sentences. Later I can expand on complex sentences, short impacting sentences, and run-ons.

Next, we code for beginnings of sentences. My students place a box around the first word of each of their sentences. Then they pull those words out onto another piece of paper and list them in their order of use. It does not take long for students to see when they have repeated the same word over and over. I can now model lessons on changing sentences around, sentence-combining, and varying sentence beginnings. An unexpected lesson that comes from this code is students often notice their misuse of capital letters (Fig. 6.3).

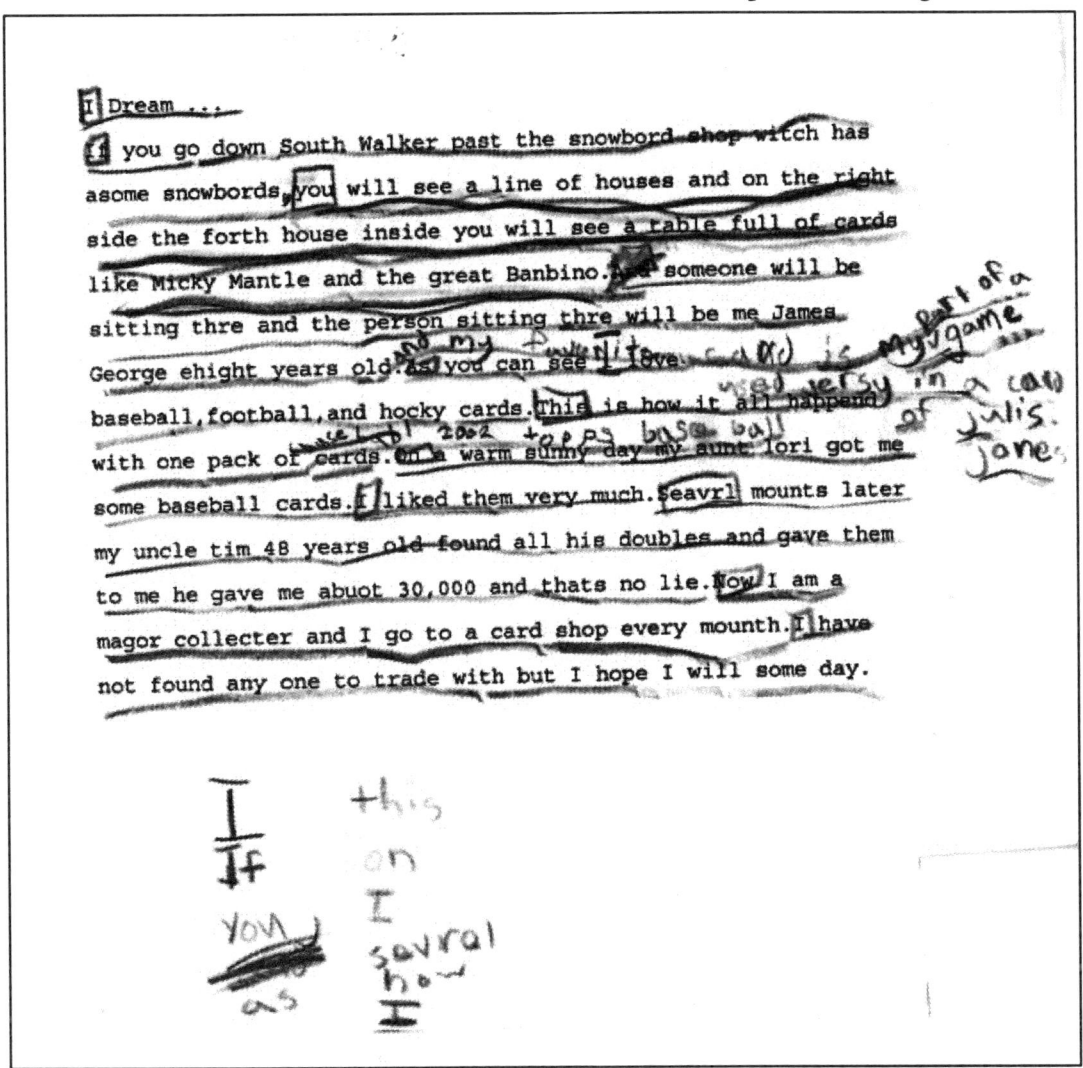

Fig. 6.3

Other things we code for are "be" verbs that show passive voice later in the year when students are ready and the over use of *very* and *a lot*. I see my students use ratiocination on their own when they get to revision. The color and the codes empower the students to recognize and revise their own writing easily (Fig. 6.4).

I wish I got a puppy

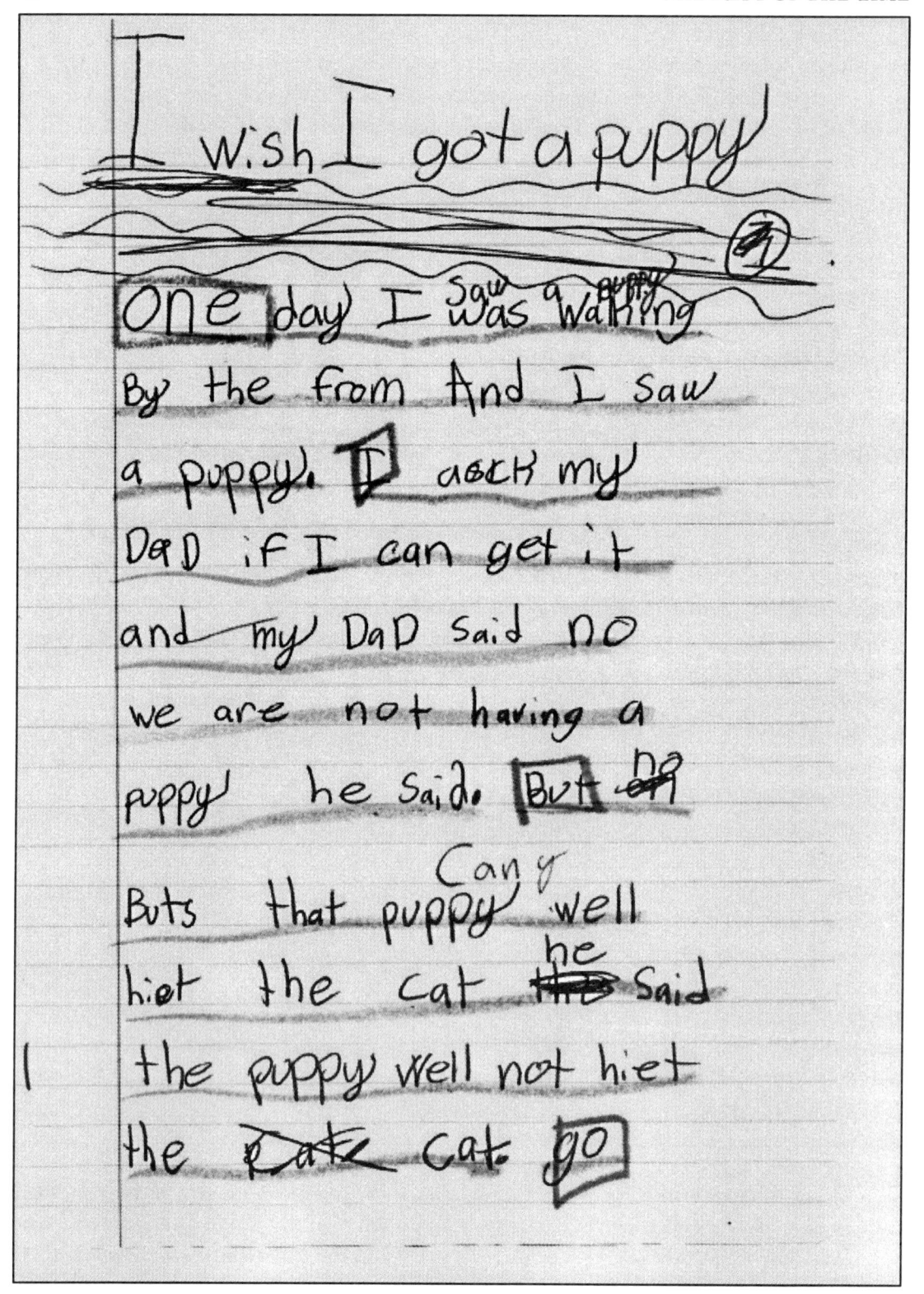

One day I saw a puppy was walking
By the from And I saw
a puppy. I asck my
DaD if I can get it
and my DaD said no
we are not having a
puppy he said. But no
Buts that puppy can y well
hiet the cat he said
the puppy well not hiet
the cat go

Fig. 6.4

Clocking

I use clocking (Carroll and Wilson 283) as an editing technique toward the end of a student's writing process after I have given the class a deadline for a completed piece of writing. Students sit in two concentric circles; this represents an analog clock. If space is sparse, students may face each other in two long lines to represent a digital clock. The students who sit in the inside circle move after each round of proofreading, so that different readers "clock" or check for different details. After my students are seated with all of the pages of the piece they are editing, from prewriting to a final copy, they take a sheet of notebook paper and write the title of their piece and their name as the author. We make three columns down the page. One for their names, one that has a drawing of eyes on it, with the words "Eyes on," and another for comments. When the students switch papers, they write their name next to the appropriate number. Then I ask them to look for—"have their eyes on"—a specific detail from a minilesson during the past few weeks. For example, we may first check that they wrote a title on their piece. That is all the first round would entail. If the student has a title, the reader writes yes, or good work, in the comments section (Figs. 6.5, 6.6) To help third graders, they number their lines on their final draft before we clock. That way when we edit for word wall words, or commas, they write down the line number they think needs to be corrected in the comments section. It makes it easier for the writer to find their mistake later. After we have proofread for everything that I think needs to be looked at, writers have the opportunity to reenter their writing to make any changes they feel are necessary. Clocking is a way for students to "consider one concept or detail at a time, so they focus more intently on it rather than trying to do everything at once—or nothing at all" (Carroll & Wilson 283).

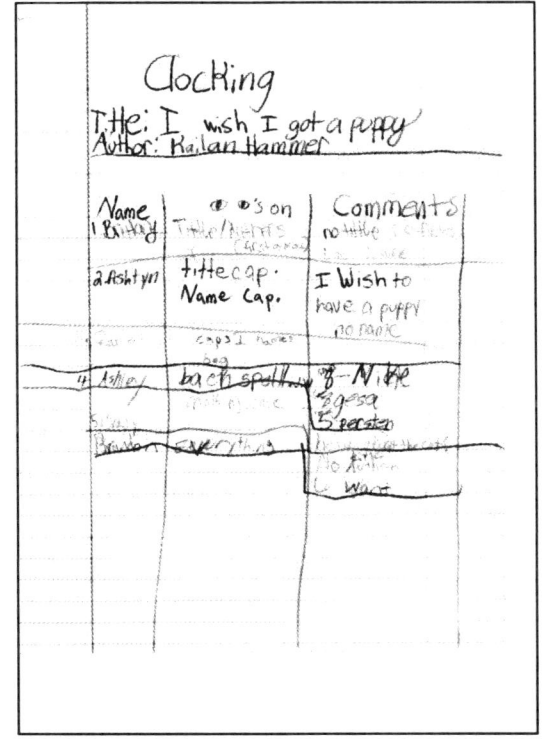

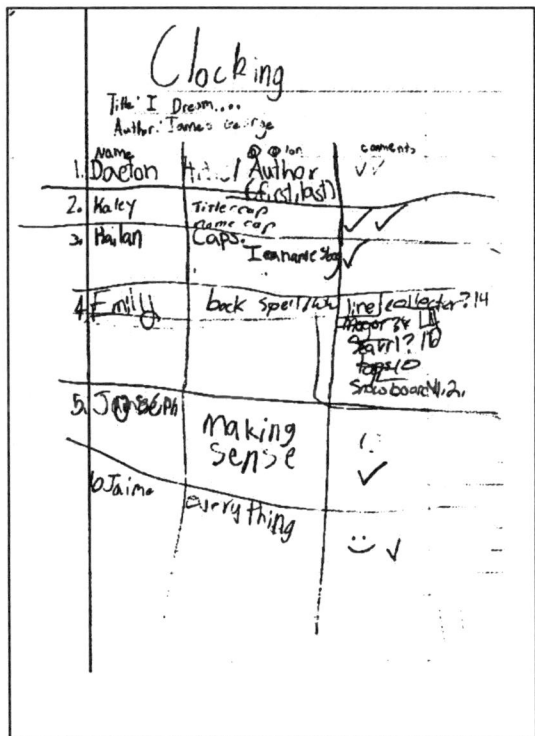

Fig. 6.3

Fig. 6.3

Commas

One of the comma rules I teach, the easiest I feel for third graders, is commas in a series. Around Thanksgiving everyone has the students write what they are thankful for. I read *Humble Pie* by Jennifer Donnelly. Theo, the main character, learns the important lesson of not taking things for granted and appreciating what he has in life. When we finish the story, we make a list of things for which Theo is thankful. I model how to turn the list into two or three sentences using commas in a series. *Theo is thankful for his mom, his dad, his brother, and his sister. He appreciates his cow, his chicken, and the cat.* We discuss the word humble and then thankful. We come up with the synonyms of *appreciative* and *grateful* as alternatives to repeating "I am thankful" over and over. My students make a list of everything they are thankful for. They create a turkey out of construction paper. Then, using my model as an example, they create sentences from their list of thankful items and place them on the turkey. I laminate their work to take home and share with their family. As I walk around to assess, I check that they understood how to correctly use commas in a series, and then I hold them accountable for correct usage in their future writing.

Other Lessons

Triptych

Even though many of my students have never heard of the word *triptych* before this lesson, they immediately see it as having to do with three because of the words *triple* and *triplet*. I always start by telling the origins of the triptych in history because it is fascinating. "The triptych comes from ancient, hinged, three-leaved tablets and three-paneled tapestries. Because people had no means for hanging one enormous picture, they would divide it into three sections so that each section could be hung individually. By mounting them close together on a wall, the picture could be viewed as a whole". (Carroll & Wilson 195) I have a triptych of a nativity scene carved in wood that I bring as an example.

In *Acts of Teaching*, the triptych lesson focuses on subject verb agreement. When making this concept concrete, the students draw a picture of an animal or an object that fits across the divided three sections of the page. In the first section where the head of the object rests, the students write a noun phrase, the middle section is a verb phrase, and the last section is a prepositional phrase. Many third graders have never heard of these grammatical terms, but when I model and practice these with them, they catch on quickly. As I was reading *Sarah, Plain and Tall* by Patricia MacLachlan to my students, I realized that I wanted to try the triptych using appositives. I model a triptych with *Sarah* in the first section, *plain and tall*, in the middle, and a verb phrase at the end. So our sentence usually ends up sounding something like: Sarah, plain and tall, moves in with her new family. Instead of lying horizontally, the triptych now lays vertically since the picture will be of a person. After I model Sarah's sentence, the students write a sentence with an appositive about themselves. When we staple all of the pages together and make a flip book, it becomes the most popular book in our library (Figs. 6.7, 6.8).

Fig. 6.7

Fig. 6.8

Descriptive Writing

I first did this descriptive writing lesson with a Halloween story, *John Pig's Halloween* by Jan Waldron. One of the pages describes the pig's costumes vividly. I conceal the picture from the students so they visualize the costume as I read the description. Then I show the students the illustration, and they see if the picture in their mind matched the one in the book. Next the students draw on a piece of white paper the costume they plan to wear for Halloween, or one that they want to wear. They also conceal their picture (Fig. 6.9). On another piece of paper, they write a description of their costume but do not tell what it is (Fig. 6.10). We hang all of the pictures at random, and I randomly pass out the descriptions. After reading the descriptions, students try to match each to a costume. This

Fig. 6.9

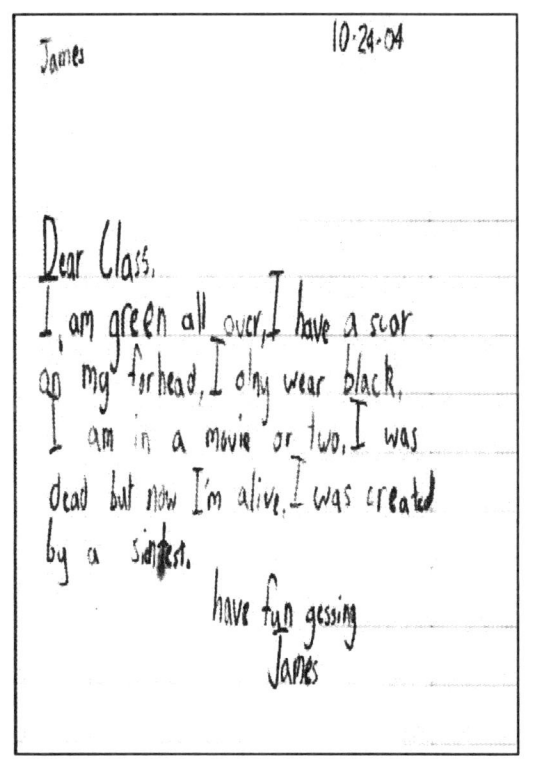

Fig. 6.10

activity really shows the students how important to writing is describing an object vividly and correctly.

I expanded this lesson by using the book *Dear Mr. Blueberry* by Simon James. Since the character sees a whale out the window, I have the students draw a big window and then behind it something they "see" out the window. They then write the description of what they see on another piece of paper. We hang the images up, read the descriptions and match them to the pictures. During writing workshop the next few days, I have them find an object or scene that needs more description in their writing and use our visualizing method to revise.

Writing Roulette

Chris Van Allsburg's books are fabulous for writing roulette lessons because of the fantasy style pictures. I use the pictures from *The Mysteries of Harris Burdick* as a prompt for writing roulette. The way I teach this lesson depends on the level of my students and their writing so far in the year. Writing roulette invites one person to start a story, the next person adds to it, and so on until the end. I have used the same *Harris Burdick* picture with all of my students and done a class version of writing roulette. I have also tiered the lesson by using multiple pictures from the story and placing students in groups where one group worked in pairs, one group wrote individually, and one wrote altogether as a group. All work. I like the pictures in *Harris Burdick* because they have a lead sentence if the students are stuck for a beginning. Because the pictures are so fantastical, the students usually have no problem being creative with their leads.

Any pictures or prompts will work for this lesson. I have done writing roulette in content areas about a subject we are studying and even in math by having the students start a word problem and add to it as they rotate the page. The students love writing roulette because of the collaboration factor. It is a lesson that must take place in a classroom where students are comfortable with each other. In third grade, some students may not have clear handwriting or be able to read each other's work, so that is when I place students in pairs or small groups to rotate.

I also use this strategy on parent night. My students create a lead sentence on chart paper before we leave for the day. As parents come to Open House, I encourage them to add to the story. I ask the last parents to write a conclusion or the students and I do it together the next day. We tried this in our office with visitors who come in each day and everyone loved it, but it is best as a learning tool for my students about transitions and coherence.

Traditions and Celebrations

Each year around Christmas, I have the students bring in an object that they use in a holiday tradition. If parents are worried about an item breaking, they can send a picture. If their tradition centers around a song or a book they read, I have them bring the words or the book. We study and read about the traditions of other countries this time of

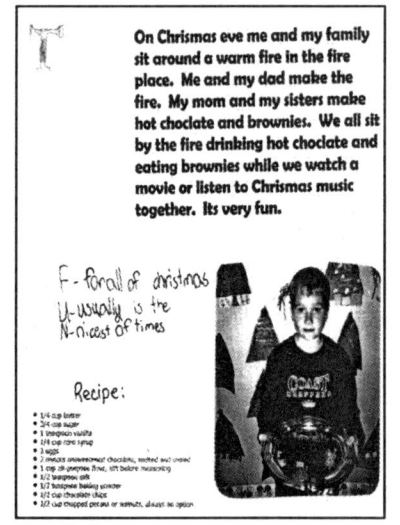

Fig. 6.11

year and their writing about their tradition becomes a memorable keepsake for years to come (Fig 6.11).

I have also had students write about a traditional celebration time they have in their family. It can be a birthday tradition or something from anytime of the year. We read *I'm in Charge of Celebrations* by Byrd Baylor.

The following lessons are still only a small portion of what is available and can be used according to your student expectations and curriculum guides.

Books I Keep in My Writing Center for Minilessons
- *Tough Cookie* by David Wisniewski—point of view (from a cookie in the cookie jar)
- *A Chocolate Moose for Dinner* by Fred Gwynne and *Mad as a Wet Hen* by Marvin Terban —figurative language
- *The Pain and the Great One* by Judy Blume—comparison/ contrast
- *Truman's Aunt Farm* by Jana Kim Rattigan—homophones like aunt and ant
- *Once There Was a Bull... (Frog)* by Rick Walton—compound words
- *Aunt Isabel Tells a Good One* by Kate Duke—story elements, writing a narrative
- *Elephants Aloft* by Kathi Apelt—prepositions
- *Four Famished Foxes and Fosdyke* by Pamela Duncan Edwards—alliteration
- *Voices in the Park* by Anthony Browne—voice, characterization, and point of view
- *Many Luscious Lollipops* by Ruth Heller—teaching adjectives
- *A Mink, a Fink, a Skating Rink What Is a Noun?* By Brian P. Cleary—teaching nouns
- *How Writers Work, Poetry Matters,* and *A Writer's Notebook* all by Ralph Fletcher—Fletcher writes these chapter books in a kid friendly manner to explain certain parts of the writing workshop.
- *If You Were a Writer* by Joan Lowery Nixon, Author *A True Story* by Helen Lester, and *If •You Give an Author a Pencil* by Laura Numeroff—stories of writers' writing processes
- *From Pictures to Words A Book About Making A Book* by Janet Stevens and *Look at My Book How Kids Can Write & Illustrate Terrific Books* by Loreen Leedy—the writing process
- *Alphabet Under Construction* by Denise Fleming and *The Alphabet Keeper* by Mary Murphy—introduce rearranging letters to make new words
- *The Art Lesson* by Tomie DePaola—taking risks, creating and publishing
- *Love is a Handful of Honey* by Giles Andreae and *Porcupining: A Prickly Love Story* by Lisa Wheeler—can be read around Valentine's Day as examples of figurative language
- *The Wonderful Happens* by Cynthia Rylant—listing the wonderful things in your life, adding details and expanding ideas
- *Quick as a Cricket* by Audrey Wood - similes

7 Time to Connect

"We all have our time machines. Some take us back, they're called memories. Some take us forward, they're called dreams."
Jeremy Irons

I believe that reading and writing cannot be taught separately. Students want to not only talk about what they have read, but also share in writing and reflections what they are thinking about as they read. From the first few weeks of school through my read-alouds, I begin talking about and modeling the type of connections that readers make when engaged with their text: text to self, text to text, and text to world. (Harvey & Goudvis 68)

First, I talk about what *text* is because that may be a new term for many students. I do this often on the same day I do my lesson from the first twenty one days about "What does writing look like?" They begin to realize that text is anything written and comes in many different forms, not just as books. We connect this immediately to writing and what they have already begun to write in their writer's notebooks—text-to-self connections. When a book triggers a memory and they write based on that memory, it is a connection they have made. Any connection I make in talking about what I have read can then be transferred to paper, so I have them practice that. My students read for at least 30 minutes each day in what I call independent reading time. This is separate from the instructional reading time where I teach and we read together. Independent reading allows them to choose the material they want to read, practice their fluency through easier books, and enjoy different genres. While they read, I ask them to place a post-it® in their book where they have made a connection. We then share these with each other.

Most of the students will ask for time to go to their writer's notebooks to add that connection so they will have it there later perhaps to expand on in story form. I ask them to do this same thing when reading at home too. Once a week they write a reading journal letter to me where they talk about a book they have read that past week and the connections or thinking they did about the book. I have modeled example after example during reading time with books I have read, so they know what a friendly letter looks like and what I am expecting. I have 4-5 students turn in a journal each day and I write back to them. I want them to know that I value their reading experiences and am interested in what they have to say about the books they are reading.

After reading the pages in Nanci Atwell's *In the Middle* where she talks about dinner talk, I decided I wanted that same atmosphere in my classroom, where students learn "what good writers do, what good readers do, how readers of literature think and talk, what books are good for, and how kids can get in on it" (263). The students have the choice one day a week to bring in the book they wrote about and share it with the class. We chart those books so that other students can then choose one at a later time if the book recommendation seemed interesting. The students pick books sometime that I have not ever read, and that becomes another topic to write about when I reply to their letter. (Figs. 7.1, 7.2, 7.3, 7.4)

> Sep, 12, 2004
>
> Dear Mrs. Johnson,
> I didn't finish the book Junie B. Jones and the stupid smelly bus. The book was written by Barbara Park. I wonder why Barbara Park's books sometimes says my name is Junie B. Jones the B. ic stands for Beatrice. and geet like B and thats all.?
> I read the caper metting Mrs. It was funny because Mrs was laughing at the

Fig. 7.1

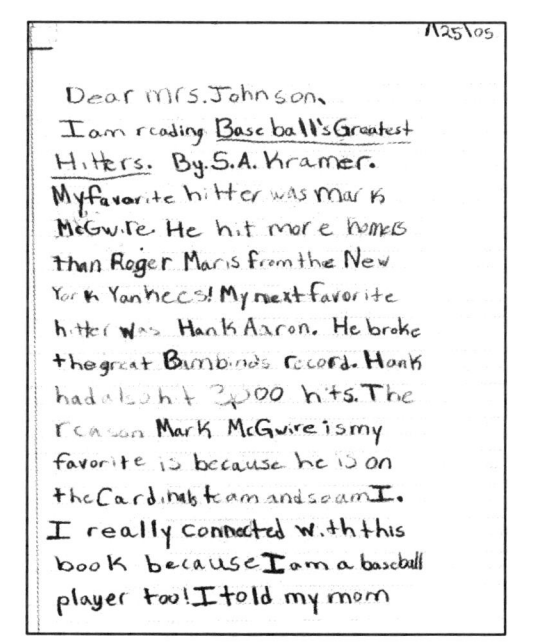

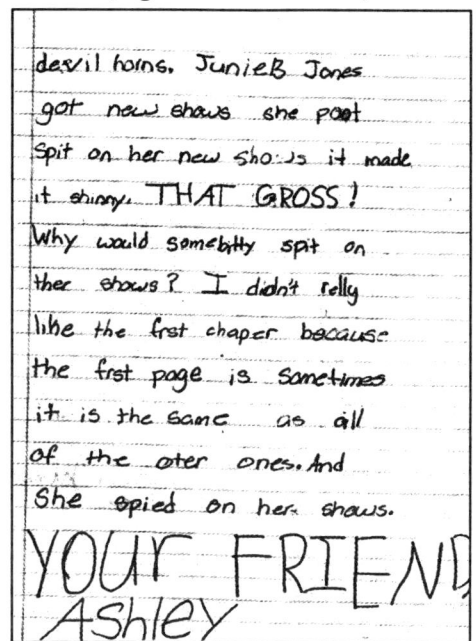

> devil horns. Junie B. Jones got new shows she poot spit on her new shows it made it shinny. THAT GROSS! Why would somebtty spit on ther shows? I didn't relly like the frst chaper because the frst page is sometimes it is the same as all of the oter ones. And she spied on her shows.
>
> YOUR FRIEND
> Ashley

Fig. 7.2

> 1/25/05
>
> Dear Mrs. Johnson,
> I am reading Baseball's Greatest Hitters. By S.A. Kramer. My favorite hitter was Mark McGwire. He hit more homers than Roger Maris from the New York Yankees! My next favorite hitter was Hank Aaron. He broke the great Bambino's record. Hank had about 3,000 hits. The reason Mark McGwire is my favorite is because he is on the Cardinals team and so am I. I really connected with this book because I am a baseball player too! I told my mom

Fig. 7.3

> that I would grow up to play baseball and preach. She said I would be a breacher. That is a baseball playing preacher. I thought that was funny. Baseball players donate money to child abuse. Someday I want to do the same.
>
> Sincerely,
> Brady

Fig. 7.4

I also know that many state tests require responses to literature. Third grade is definitely not too young to start learning more in depth ways to respond to text. One such activity that we learn in the NJWPT/Abydos writing institute that comes from *Acts of Teaching* is the Pentad (Carroll and Wilson 76).

During the first weeks of school in social studies as we study character education using classroom rules, I read *Stand Tall, Molly Lou Melon* by Patty Lovell. After we have done a reading/wriitng connection, we share times when we feel confident or how it feels to be teased as Molly Lou Melon experienced, I teach the pentad. The purpose of the pentad, as stated in *Acts of Teaching*, is to "minimize rambling" and "dramatize or emphasize the focus" of a text. It "helps students come closer to uncovering the human motives of the "drama" (76). My students do not always understand what a drama is, even though they choose to be overly dramatic at times.

The pentad introduces the students to the elements of drama while helping them create an analysis that facilitates comprehension. I model on the board the five parts of the pentad, writing on pieces that will eventually form the final star when they come together. I teach the students that the actors are the characters. Next we move to the scenes, which are the settings of the story, and then the acts, or what happened in the story. In the case of Molly Lou Melon, she has to use her unique traits to stand tall like her grandmother taught her. The agencies, or how she stood tall, would be when she sang out, stacked pennies on her teeth, and created the most beautiful snowflake in the class. Her purpose, or why she did those things, was to show Ronald Durkin, the bully, that her uniqueness was an asset not a hindrance. When we put the five parts together, they form a star. This creates coherence throughout the story and becomes a visual story map. Later, students use that same concept in their own writing as they plan a new piece. The students choose one piece of the pentad that they would like to write about. This ensures depth. We discuss afterwards that when they wrote, many times they included other pieces from the pentad as well. I tell them, "You have written your first literary analysis as an eight year old."

In September, my team sponsors a grandparent breakfast in honor of Grandparent's Day. We use our instructional reading time to read books with grandparents as the main character. We integrate numerous reading and writing skills into these two weeks. We learn what an adjective is and practice by creating a chart of each grandparent character, adjectives that describe him or her, and a short summary or connection to remember the story. Later the students use what they know about adjectives to create a grandparent acrostic that we share whole class at the breakfast.

We also begin a short Quicklist about our own family members, including our grandparents. The students write memories about their own grandparents with a little prompting from the books and charts we have made. I read *When I Was Young in the Mountains* by Cynthia Rylant. Using the book as a model, I write short vignettes of when I was young with my grandparents. I write about my grandmother's diamond anniversary necklace that I always admired and how she cooked a twenty-five pound turkey at Thanksgiving even if there were only going to be four of us there. The students can also choose to write short vignettes of a few memories instead of just one they remember. They use their writing workshop time to take their grandparent story through the writing process. Some choose to create fictional stories using their grandparents as well.

Another activity we include is based on *Thunder Cake* by Patricia Polacco, discussing recipe words and then writing a recipe for the perfect grandparent (Fig. 7.5).

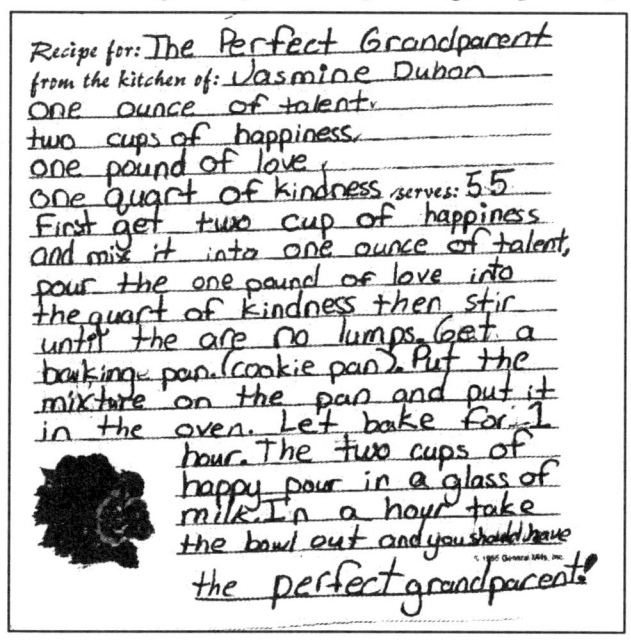

Fig. 7.5

The students may interview their grandparents and create a Venn Diagram comparing themselves to their grandparents (Figs. 7.6, 7.7). These all become treasures for families throughout the years.

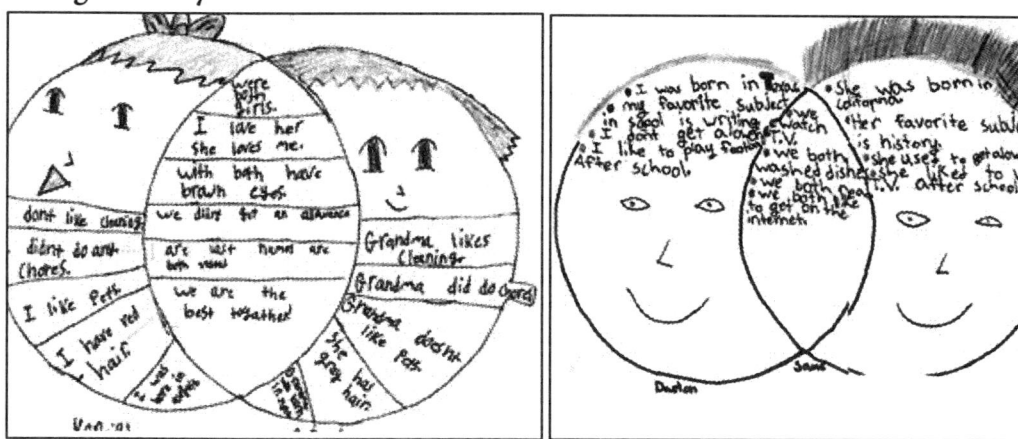

Fig. 7.6   Fig. 7.7

Students who do not have a grandparent that can attend the breakfast by serving the food and being my special helper; or, if they wish, they may "adopt" another teacher or the principal to enjoy the breakfast with them. An aunt or other family member may also attend. I have never had a student whose grandparents were all deceased, but should that happen, I would encourage the family to write down memories and enjoy a discussion of their family history.

Pumpkin Characters

Also during the fall months, my students choose a favorite character from a book and create a pumpkin model of it. They do this as an at-home family project. If real pumpkins are too expensive or you want to do this in class, they can create character pumpkins out of paper. The students bring in their chosen book, share it with the class, explain why they like it, and why or how they connect to the character.

Author Studies

Susan Stevens Crummell writes books with her sister, Janet Stevens that I love to read to my students. A book of theirs that I discovered this past year is *Plaidypus Lost.* It is about a stuffed toy, a platypus made out of plaid that keeps getting lost. It is written in rhyme and repetition. As we read, text-to-self connections flow freely, and then the students start realizing the text-to-text connections with *Corduroy* by Don Freeman, *The Velveteen Rabbit* by Margery Williams, and *The Doll People* by Ann Matthews Martin. I have my students bring their favorite toy from home, and I bring Raggedy Ann, my doll from childhood. They then categorize themselves by their toy. We may have a doll group, an animal group, action figures, balls, and transportation.

Their activity for writing workshop time was to plan out a story using their toys as a part of the main action or as the main character. This is creativity at its best! Some of the students did a companion story to *Plaidypus Lost* and wrote about being at a birthday party and having someone steal their dolls while they played. One group used their toy cars in a story about a big race. After a few days of drafting and working through the process, the groups shared their stories. Many of the students later went on to write an individual story about their toy (Fig. 7.8).

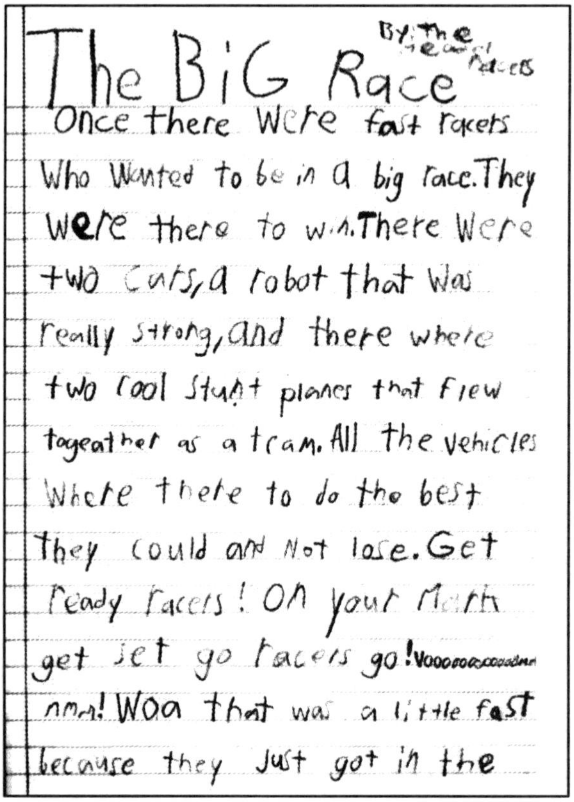
The BiG Race
By: The ... Racers
Once there Were fast racers Who Wanted to be in a big race. They were there to win. There Were two Cars, a robot that Was really strong, and there where two cool Stunt planes that flew togeather as a team. All the vehicles Where there to do the best they could and Not lose. Get ready racers! On your Mark get set go racers go! Vooooooooooom! Woa that was a little fast because they just got in the

Fig. 7.8

One of the other Susan Stevens Crummel books that I use is *Cook a Doodle Do*. The characters cook up a new recipe for strawberry shortcake with lots of mishaps and fun in between. We create a recipe for a class cake and then make party hats to wear. We connect this book to a time in our life when we have celebrated or hosted a party. The students sit in their party hats and write up a storm. We wear our hats and have party blowers as we listen to each person share.

Another book of theirs, *And the Dish Ran Away with the Spoon*, is a perfect introduction to nursery rhymes and a fantasy genre unit.

One more author that we study when I introduce writing about memories and family stories from life is Patricia Polacco. All of her books portray characters from her family or her childhood, and she is famous for taking a special moment and creating a story around it. Her books are the model I use for the memoir genre.

An additional reading/writing unit I do focuses on *Charlotte's Web* by E.B. White. With multiple characters involved in the plot, the opportunity for the teaching of character traits, motivations, and feelings arises. After reading a few chapters and learning the identities of the main characters, the students choose a character they would like to follow throughout the book. Being a childhood favorite with its own video version, many of the students have already read or seen *Charlotte's Web*. Because of that, I encourage the students to think more deeply about the characters E.B. White created and his use of language and voice.

The lessons I teach with this book can be done with any book. I use them as a starting point to our reading time. While listening to the story, the students keep sticky notes in hand and mark pages that have special importance to them, pages they want to return to later. After we share our sticky notes, we move directly into integrating the same lessons into the composition we are working on at the moment. This is a time when the students see author's craft and apply it to their own writing.

I begin the first day of this novel study with a lesson on adjectives, specifically describing possible emotions a character experiences. On an anchor chart, the students brainstorm as many feeling words as they can recall. After the list is exhausted, we begin to look for those words as we read. This is an appropriate time to start talking to the students about inferences. The author is not always going to directly say that the character is angry or sad. In the next few lessons we will discover other ways an author may describe the feelings of the character.

The next day, after having written down on index cards the feeling words the students generated as well as adding a few of my own, I pass out the cards randomly to the students. Our lesson will focus on sorting the feelings into groups. This leads into our discussion of synonyms. We may have ten different words that are substitutes for happy. We can then use the cards to make webs of feeling words and their synonyms that will stay in our Writing Tools folder all year. We continue this lesson by using a visual to talk about depth of emotion. I choose three basic feeling words, such as *happy*, *sad*, and *mad*. On the board I write four of the synonyms we discussed the day before.

Then we make a linear array for those words, which in Janet Allen's *Words, Words, Words*, she describes as "visual representations of degree" (52). For example, for *mad*, I write *furious*, *annoyed*, *upset*, and *angry*. I give examples of how these words are different degrees of the same feeling. I may be *upset* for a few minutes but then get over it. If I am *furious*, I may fume over the problem for days. The students' arrays are the visual representation of what they see as the degree of their own emotions. After this lesson, the students became experts at picking this out of *Charlotte's Web*. In one chapter, the paragraph deals with Wilbur and the flies that are bothering him. White writes about the animals feelings toward the flies using the words *hate, detest, annoy,* and *pester*. Later, when describing Wilbur's feelings about death, White uses the words *kill, murder,* and *butcher*. Both times the students heard the synonyms and reacted by pointing them out.

By this time in the novel, we have seen the author show his characters' feelings through their actions. On one page early in the book White writes that Fern "sobbed." I ask the students what that means. Why would someone sob? This question leads into a discussion of the different times people cry. They could be upset, angry, or joyful. We look at the context of Fern's action. Why is she crying? This is a great time to reinforce the strategy of inference. The students then draw four squares on their paper. They write a feeling word in each quadrant. I usually model with sad because of Fern's actions in the book. I ask the students to brainstorm verbs. How does a person show they are sad? The usual responses are crying, hanging their head down, pouting, or frowning. We repeat this listing with anger, happiness, and feeling frightened. Now, the students are able to recognize these actions when they hear them, and also show action in their own writing instead of being so literal.

In another lesson, I read *Yesterday I Had the Blues* by Jeron Ashford Frame or *The Sunday Blues* by Neal Layton. Figurative language creates an image for the reader. I want the students to have as many tools for language as I can teach them. Usually the students have heard of a few connections of color to emotion, like red for anger and blue for depression. This book goes through the colors of yellow, gray, and pink among others. Another book that uses color to portray emotion is *My Many Colored Days* by Dr. Seuss. If I want to add another synonym lesson that deals with color here, students make color wheels and find other words for everyday colors they use to describe objects in their writing.

Reading *Hailstones and Halibut Bones* by Mary O'Neill, a poetry collection of colors, adds to the students' knowledge of figurative language with similes and metaphors. Other books to be used in conjunction with minilessons on color are *Get Red!* and *Blue Aliens!* both by Tony Porto. I have used the whimsical *Wait! No Paint* by Bruce Whatley, pitting three pigs against an illustrator who runs out of red paint, as an illustration of the impact color can make on a storyline. These lessons would not necessarily need to be in conjunction with *Charlotte's Web*, but may be added in as minilessons that coincide with using colors and emotions in writing.

After the students have connected all the feelings activities with character traits and motivations, we begin to trace memories of times in our own life when we have experienced those same emotions. I read *Today I Feel Silly* by Jamie Lee Curtis. We pull out examples from the book of what the author does to provide examples for each emotion. She may include details, use synonyms, or add action. The students immediately realize that these are the same strategies presented in the past few revision lessons. I give them three index cards to begin with. On the first index card, they choose an emotion that they identify with and write it at the top. For about three minutes, they write anything they want to about that emotion. They may choose to write, as Jamie Lee Curtis did, about a time in their life when they felt as she did. They may list synonyms, similes, or verbs to fit that emotion or do a mixture of both. We do this with three different emotions. Then we loop the three index cards together with string and the students may illustrate on the back of the card a scene from their writing. This becomes prewriting to be kept in their Writing Tools folder for the rest of the year. Many of the students choose to use something from this lesson as a story starter; some have turned these quick writes in to a poem (Figs. 7.9, 7.10).

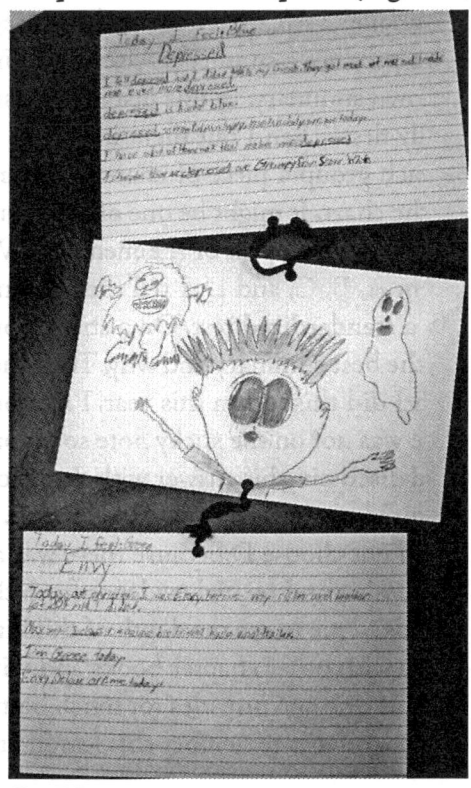

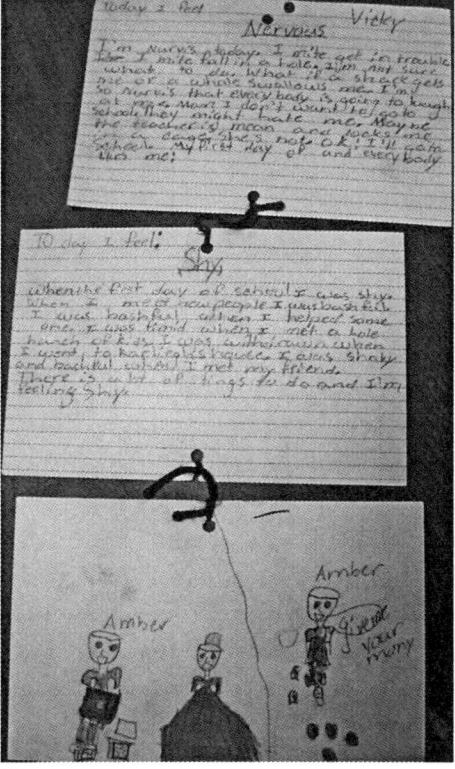

Fig. 7.9

Fig. 7.10

To finish up this unit on imagery and characterization in both reading and writing, I use Joyce Armstrong Carroll's "Prove Its" from *Writing with Depth* (2). On the third page of *When Sophie Gets Angry, Really, Really Angry* by Molly Bang it says "Sophie was really angry." I stop there and ask the kids to prove that Sophie was angry. Just because the author has made a statement, simply told us something, should we believe it? We have to show, not just tell the readers that Sophie was angry. I encourage them to think back on our lessons surrounding emotion. After they have written a few ideas down, we write new sentences on the board proving that Sophie really was angry. She stomped her feet, kicked and screamed. Steam poured from her ears. The students add many details. We then go back to the book and see what the author wrote to show that she was angry. The kids love when they have some of the same thoughts as the author. Bang writes, "She roars a red, red roar. Sophie is a volcano ready to explode." After these lessons connecting their reading to their writing, I begin to see a much stronger grasp of language in their compositions. We transferred these lessons into a "feeling" composition where they actually started a piece about a time they were scared, bored, excited—their choice. The subject of emotions in their own life becomes a topic many explore through different forms of writing the rest of the year. Another great book to use with Prove Its and showing emotions is *Leonardo the Terrible Monster* by Mo Willems.

At the end of our lessons on theme and characterization with *Charlotte's Web*, I read *Peach & Blue* by Sarah S. Kilborne. The students draw many text to text connections around the theme of friendship between these two characters and the emotions dealing with the concept of dying.

Not only do we work on characterization with *Charlotte's Web*, we engage in the strategy of using the beginning, middle, and end of a chapter to produce a summary. After modeling summaries of a few chapters, the students write their own summary. In this instance, I used chapter 14, *Dr. Dorian*. The students write individually first. Then I put them in groups to compare summaries and discuss each others. I give each group a piece of chart paper and they choose the summary that they want to write on the chart. It might be one of the group members' summaries or it could be a new summary decided on by all of the members. We hang the four charts up on the board and I label them A, B, C, and D. I tell the students that this is the way a summary question may look on a standardized test. On a sticky note, each student writes down which answer they think is the best summary and why. Then they go stick it up on the summary of their choices. When I did this lesson this year, I had one student place his sticky note on summary D. His name was not on the sticky note so no one knew it was his except me. I asked him if he would mind discussing his answer with the whole group. He didn't. He had written that D was the best summary because it was the longest. A teachable moment was upon us. The other students did not choose D because there was an unimportant detail added on at the end. Through discussion and textual evidence from the chapter, students decided which answer was best. It amazed me to see the depth of thinking produced in the students' summaries. I use this activity with other chapter books and with picture books. Using hands on, thinking activities such as this one provides for much better preparation of standardized tests than a worksheet. My students remember this lesson and apply it now to their thinking as they read.

To capitalize on this success with beginning, middle, and end summaries, we use this strategy as a peer conferencing tool on a work in progress. The students chose a partner to read their piece to, a classmate they feel comfortable with. The partner listens and writes down what he or she heard as the beginning, the middle, and the end—a summary of the composition. If the partner's summary matches the original intention of the author, then they repeat the process with the partner's piece. If not, they discuss the differences to see where the miscommunication happened. Trust occurs through daily reading and writing together, and this activity maintains a level of respect where everyone enjoys success. A lesson like this one is another bridge between a reading strategy and the students' writing processes.

A book I use toward the end of the year with my third graders is *Rope Burn* by Jan Siebold. The author has titled each of the chapters with a proverb, like "Haste Makes Waste" or "A Penny Saved is a Penny Earned". At the beginning of this read-aloud, I introduce the students to each proverb from the book. I mix them up so they are not in the order of the chapters. We discuss if they have heard the proverb before, what a proverb is, and what these mean. We make connections to help them retain this new knowledge. Then as I read a chapter from the book, the students guess which proverb matches that chapter. They must use textual evidence from the chapter to support their claim. This activity requires a depth of thinking from the concrete to the abstract, the literal to the figurative. After we have read the entire book, the students choose one of the proverbs to write about in connection to something from their own life.

Here are three other reading and writing connections that I love to share with my students:

The Secret Remedy Book by Karin Cates is about a little girl who goes to visit her aunt and becomes homesick. Her aunt shares with her the secret remedies for adventure and fun. My students create a class book of their own secret remedies.

The Book of Bad Ideas by Laura Huliska-Beith is a great way to have a little fun with the rules. After reading the book, we generate a list of things we would do at school that would be a bad idea, like throwing things, calling names, or chewing gum. We make a class book that we revisit when we need a reminder of good and bad behavior.

The last one is *Grandpa's Teeth* by Rod Clements about a dog who steals his owner's teeth. I like reading this to begin our class mystery unit because it shows the students that we have to look closely at everything to find clues and suspects.

More Reading and Writing Connections

10-Step Guide to Living With Your Monster by Laura Numeroff—writing instructions

Substitute Teacher Plans by Doug Johnson—to leave for a substitute to read

School Picture Day by Lynn Plourde and *Crazy Hair Day* by Barney Saltzberg—text to self connections, an anxious or memorable day

How To Lose All Your Friends by Nancy Carlson—a how-to guide

How to be a Practically Perfect Pig by Nick Ward—a how-to guide, manners

The Hard Times Jar by Ethel Footman Smothers—writing about tough times

Ordinary Mary's Extraordinary Deed—writing about good deeds

A Box of Friends by Pam Munoz Ryan—missing someone. special keepsakes

You Don't Always Get What You Hope For by Rick Walton—wishes, getting what you want versus what you deserve

Diary of a Worm by Doreen Cronin—journaling and keeping a diary or schedule of your day; point of view

The Black Snowman by Phil Mendez—I read this book in the winter time in conjunction with "Frosty the Snowman" to make a venn diagram and text to text connections

Sylvester and the Magic Pebble by William Steig—using your wishes wisely

> **Books That Foster the Love of Reading**
>
> *Who's Afraid of the Big Bad Book?* By Lauren Child
> *Beware of the Storybook Wolves* by Lauren Child
> *Mrs. Goodstory* by Joy Cowley
> *The Best Place to Read* by Debbie Bertram
> *A Story For Bear* by Dennis Haseley
> *A Quiet Place* by Douglas Wood
> *Book* by George Ella Lyon
> *Book! Book! Book!* By Deborah Bruss
> *I Hate to Read* by Rita Marshall

In any classroom, reading and writing must go hand-in-hand for optimal learning to occur. Reading enhances the writing process and writing maximizes meaning of text. Students need to be challenged in the development of their own writing through the process of learning author's craft within daily literature exposure.

8 Time for Everything Else

"Don't say you don't have enough time. You have exactly the same number of hours per day that were given to Helen Keller, Pasteur, Michelangelo, Mother Teresa, Leonardo DaVinci, Thomas Jefferson, and Albert Einstein."
H. Jackson Brown, Jr.

Reading and writing workshop and all that I have talked about so far represent only a sixth of my day. My curriculum requires me to cover other subjects as well. I do as much writing as possible in those other subjects. It helps the students learn more and grasp the concepts with a little more ease.

Math

I use either the first or last 15 minutes of my math time to journal. If I want to know what they already understand before we start, I ask them some leading questions. They may be as simple as, "How do you subtract? Describe a triangle to me, or write out an addition word problem for your neighbor to solve." Some days I need to check for understanding of a lesson we just completed, and we do a quick write where they may tell me what they learned in their own words. I also read stories to them about shapes or numbers or other math ideas, so that even in math I am modeling reading and writing. Then we may write a story using a math concept as a character. I also use writing roulette in math to allow collaboration on writing word problems.

To foster a love of poetry for those who may be more mathematically inclined, for each new math concept we cover, I choose poems to share from *Math For All Seasons* by Greg Tang, *Marvelous Math A Book Of Poems* by Lee Bennett Hopkins, and *Counting Caterpillars and Other Math Poems* by Betsy Franco.

Science

"Matter" was always a concept that took a little longer for my students to grasp because it's taught at the beginning of the year. The meaning of vocabulary terms in content areas is sometimes different than the meaning in language arts. When we first discuss the scientific use of the word "matter," we also talk about the other meanings and ways we use the word. For example, students say, "What is the matter with you?" or a teacher might say, "I will take that matter under advisement." This discussion is a quick way to incorporate a multi-meaning words lesson in a subject other than language arts. As a team, we decide to begin our science year with a fun experiment and a reading/writing connection that would help the students discuss matter in a meaningful way.

Oobleck Experiment and Matter

As we learn about the concept of solids, liquids, and gasses, we begin to talk about each category's physical properties. This is a perfect time to teach adjectives and more descriptive writing. We brainstorm physical properties under each category, like hard for a solid, or flowing for a liquid. The students use their descriptions to write riddles about an object they have chosen. If they choose an apple, there riddle might be, "It is a solid. It is red. It is edible". They share with each other and try to guess.

Toward the end of the "matter" unit, I read *Bartholomew Cubbins and the Oobleck* by Dr. Seuss. We stop on the page where the oobleck begins to fall. We then make oobleck as a class or in small groups depending on how many parent volunteers I have. The recipe I use is cornstarch, water, and green food coloring. After we have experimented with and observed our oobleck, we do some writing about what we think will happen to the kingdom in the story if this oobleck were to fall. Later we finish the story and see if our predictions were correct. We talk about the "matter" that does fall from the sky in the form of weather and talk about the benefits of each type of matter and the disastrous results some matter causes, such as hail. The students then write about the whole experience and add the pictures I've taken of them with the "goop" as a day to remember (Fig. 8.1).

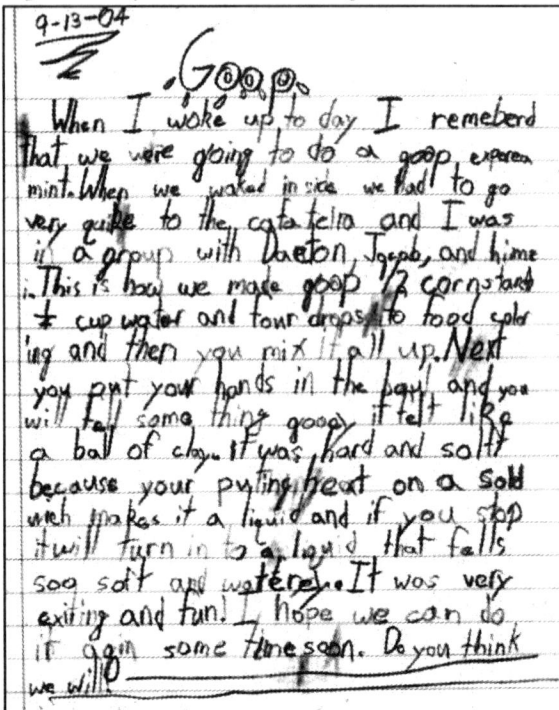

Fig. 8.1

Natural Disasters

In my school we create a library unit around our science or social studies student expectations. This allows for one more way to integrate reading, writing, and research. After the tsunami hit the continent of Asia in December of 2004, my students asked me a million questions about what causes a tsunami, and they wondered if it could happen here. My colleagues and I decided to focus our unit on natural disasters, their causes and effects. We pulled books off of our library shelves and let the students choose the disaster they would research based on availability of information. Our librarian taught lessons on nonfiction structures of text, glossaries, finding information on the Internet, and taking notes. Every day the students had time to research and answer questions they had about their disaster. Each group of students wrote a chapter detailing what they had learned. We put all of the chapters together into a bound class book for the nonfiction area of our classroom library.

The Solar System

Another research unit we do is based on the solar system. Our student expectations focus on the sun and its planets. After choosing a planet and numerous days of research, the students construct a travel brochure persuading someone to visit their planet. I find travel brochures from the Internet and agencies around town for the students to use as models. They realize how important it is to include facts about their planet, as well as opinions and exaggerations to convince a traveler their planet is the best. A book that works well with this unit by turning nonfiction and biographical facts into rhyme is *Man on the Moon* by Anastasia Suen.

Seasons

After visiting the planetarium in our city and watching a show on how the rotation of the earth effects our seasons, I taught a prewriting strategy that I thought worked well with what they had learned. I read *The Old Woman Who Loved to Read* by John Winch which talks about a woman who moves to the country and watches as the seasons change. We divided a piece of paper into quadrants to represent each season. We brainstormed things that happen in each season and listed them in the matching quadrant. We started with weather changes, the holidays or celebrations, sports activities, and then special memories we held from each season. We had a plethora of big ideas we could now choose to write about, plus it took a science concept from the abstract level to a more concrete level for the students to remember.

Social Studies

Character Education and Following the Rules

The first few weeks of school, we do daily lessons on building our character. The students make a book we call "Words to Live By" or another name of their choosing. Each day I read a picture book whose theme centers around a character trait. The students write what that character trait means to them, a connection or time when they displayed that trait, and then how the character exhibited that same trait in the book. Books I have used are: *Chrysanthemum* by Kevin Henkes for caring, *Smoky Night* by Eve Bunting for respect, *Stand*

Tall, Molly Lou Melon by Patty Lovell for courage, *Alexander and the Terrible, Horrible, No Good, Very Bad Day* by Judith Viorst or *The Turtle and the Hare* for perseverance, *The Empty Pot* by Demi for honesty, and *Strega Nona* by Tomie de Paola for responsibility and self discipline (Fig. 8.2, 8.3).

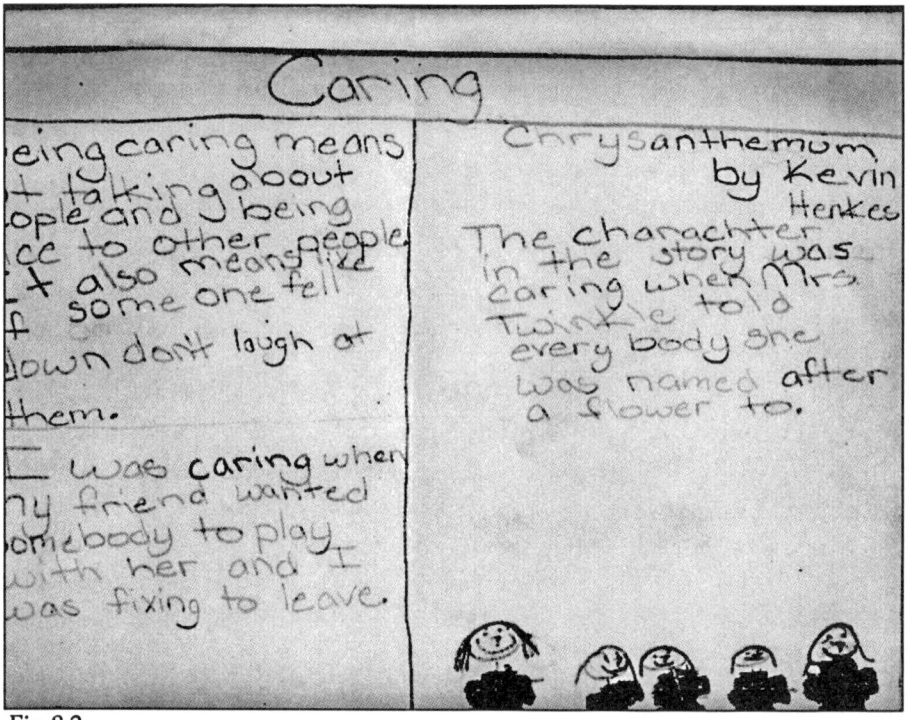

Fig. 8.2

Fig. 8.3

War

When we do our author study of Patricia Polacco, we read *The Butterfly*, which is about World War II, and *Pink and Say*, which deals with The Civil War. I do not go too in depth about each because of the young age of third graders, but we discuss civil rights and compare the times and characters in each story. These two books evoke emotions, and my students write about how they would feel in those situations. It helps them connect not only a time in history, but a culture and attitude of fear and prejudice. We write about any experiences or stories we have been told about war, and then we write a letter to a serviceman who is overseas.

The Study of Our City

Part of my third grade curriculum is a unit of study on our city, Mesquite, Texas. This is one of the many times where I use *The Important Book* by Margaret Wise Brown as a model of pattern writing. As an evaluation and product to show what the students have learned, each student chooses an important place, person, or event in Mesquite's history. They then use the repetitive nature of Brown's pattern to add details about their choice of topic. Because this evaluation is simple and fun, the students usually choose more than one important thing and make multiple pages representing what they know.

Martin Luther King, Jr. Day

I integrate reading, writing, and social studies into lessons about famous people as much as possible. In January, I start the new semester with a unit on setting goals for the New Year. Our curriculum during these six weeks centers around Martin Luther King, Jr, so I focus my reading and content area writing on biographies. These activities can last from two days to two weeks depending on the time allowed daily.

The text of *Martin's Big Words* by Doreen Rappaport opens the door in my classroom to writing about quotes and discovering the impact of someone else's words. While reading the book out loud, I encourage the students to jot down a word or two from a quote they hear that touches them. I model an entry using one of the quotes from the story. "Everyone can be great." I connect this quote to my own life and how I was made fun of growing up because I was heavy and had buck teeth. My family always told me I had a beautiful smile, and could sing and play the piano. They always encouraged me to do or be whatever I wanted no matter what people said. Then I connected my feelings to *Stand Tall, Molly Lou Melon* by Patty Lovell, a book we read earlier in the year. I could have broadened my quote to include slavery or world issues, but I knew to start with the personal first. After choosing two other quotes from the

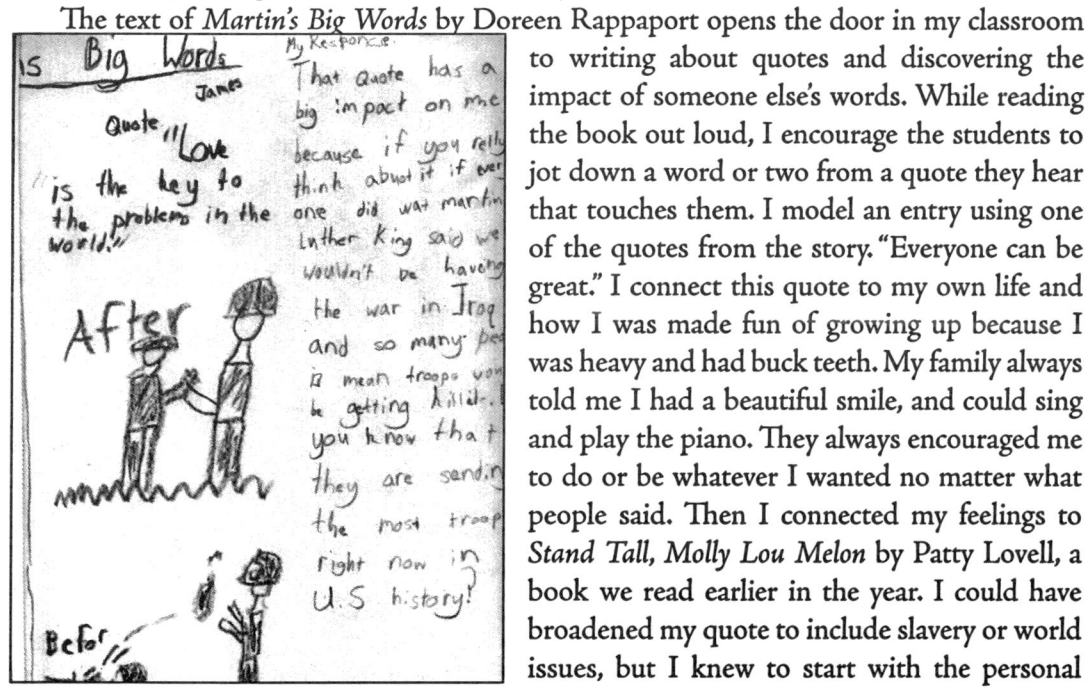

Fig. 8.4

book, the students write. In sharing, students draw powerful conclusions about each others' worlds and ideals (Fig. 8.5, 8.6). Reading a biography about Coretta Scott King during this time provides another strong role model for students.

At the top of a chart, I write the word "Dreams." The students brainstorm and free write feelings, thoughts, and ideas about that word. After about ten minutes, I put my name on the chart and write down one of my thoughts. Then each student adds his or her name and a thought. The chart becomes a multitude of different meanings and ideas about this one word. We then discuss the multiple meanings of *dream* and how the word can be used as a noun, verb, even adjective. Since we are reading biographies,

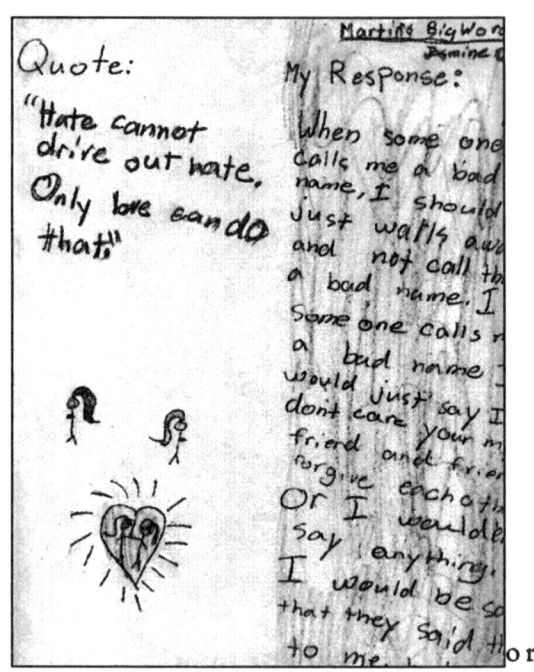

Fig. 8.5

I choose a biographical poem to read titled "Martin Luther King, Jr." by Helen H. Moore. We choral read it together to work on fluency and also take turns reading it one line at a time. We connect the word *dream* to Martin Luther King, Jr. The students usually have background knowledge on his famous speech, so we discuss what his dreams were.

I then do a paired reading with *Ruby's Wish* by Shirin Yim Bridges using information from Joyce Armstrong Carroll's reading and writing connections (www.njwpt.com). We talk about the link between Ruby, who wished to go to school, and the dream of Dr. King. I ask the students to share their thoughts on the question, "Is a wish the same as a dream?" This paired reading developed into more discussion when we added the Shel Silverstein poem "Little Abigail and the Beautiful Pony" as a third resource. Abigail became a prompt for discussing realistic wishes, hopes, and dreams, as well as the ranking of selfish wants.

Later, I read Langston Hughes poem, "Dreams." In *Strategies That Work* by Harvey and Goudvis, this poem is the anchor text for a questioning lesson (91). As we read the poem together, we ask questions and wonder. The students might not understand a word or a phrase, or I may stop and ask a question to facilitate thinking. After a discussion surrounding these three texts, the students are ready to write about their wishes and dreams, their hope for the future. I try to move them beyond, "I want to be a football player when I grow up" to more thoughtful responses and using these texts assists in reaching that goal. I believe the students leave these lessons with not only a new piece of writing, but a clearer understanding of the importance of Martin Luther King, Jr. and others like him who dreamed big and worked to make their dreams come true.

9 Assessment Time

"Nothing is a waste of time if you use the experience wisely".
Rodin

State tests and the grading system are always an issue in the classroom because they are required. In a writing process classroom, many teachers worry about being able to get grades. I have heard, *If a student is writing whatever they want all of the time, how can I grade it? How will they be able to write to a prompt on the test?* Here are some of my answers. I take grades from my minilessons at least three times a week. For example, if we are working on the skill of run on sentences and I have modeled through writing examples of complete sentences and run-on sentences, I then ask them to go back into their own writing and find a sentence they think is a run-on. They will all have one, no doubt. They highlight it, and I go around and quickly check. Sometimes they write the run-on sentence on another piece of paper and rewrite it correctly underneath. Immediately I am able to assess and tell whether that student understands the concept or not. To me, that is what grading is all about, seeing what the student understands and reteaching them if they don't. We learn how to web in the first few weeks of school. I ask that they include at least five descriptors in their web. That can be graded. If they can't think of five, then we discuss how they may not have enough information about that topic and I let them do another one. My philosophy is that it is not about failing them, but helping them do it correctly in the future. Think of Vygotsky and the famous line attributed to him, "What the child can do in cooperation today, he can do alone tomorrow" (Carroll & Wilson 317).

The same holds true for testing situations. If the students have been writing every day and see correct modeling and practice, then they know what good writing looks like. The prompt may require extra thinking time, but once they get an idea through prewriting strategies (that they will know because you have taught them), they will be able to write like they do each day in your class. All of the revising and editing strategies will be automatic. If the biggest issue for your students is staying on focus, as it is for mine, then spend extra minilesson times modeling and practicing that concept. I believe what hurts many teachers on state tests is that they try to write too much for two months before the tests and then the students are burned out or haven't learned and practiced enough. They don't get burned out when they write every day because they are enjoying it without the "two months away" pressure. Then the day of the test becomes just another writing day.

To help the students prepare for the way the state scores their writing assessment I show them the state rubric. A kid friendly version of a state assessment rubric as well as other rubrics can be found on www.suzyred.com. As we learn a new strategy to add to our writing repertoire, we also see where the use of that strategy in a composition would score points on the rubric. For example creating a prewriting web is going to help add points for organization and detail. Having a strong lead and fabulous adjectives will add to our voice. Anything concrete for the students to grasp will help them as they revise and edit a final copy.

In Texas, third-graders take a state assessment for the first time. A fellow colleague suggested that the day before the test we make a special gift for the students to take home to help ease their anxiety. We went to a dollar store and for only a few dollars bought each student a white pillowcase. That day, the students wrote good luck notes to each other on the pillowcase, words of encouragement, and strategies we had learned throughout the year. I encouraged the students to take their pillowcase home and sleep on it so their brains could soak up all of those helpful words. When the students wrote their feelings before and after the test, almost every one of them wrote about the comfort the pillowcases brought to them the night before (Fig. 9.1).

Fig. 9.1

10 Moments in Time

*"Life is a series of first time experiences - learning to ride a bike,
not to tell a big lie, coping with the dentist. There are a lot of them."*
Jan Berenstein, author of the Berenstein Bears books

Writing About Your Life, William Zinsser's latest book, became the theme in my classroom this past year through daily reflexive writing and the use of "visual literacy," otherwise known as scrapbooking.

People described me growing up as "the little girl who always had a camera." I loved taking pictures and putting them in photo albums. As I got older, I would add captions to the photos or write a name and date. Until my son was born four years ago, I did not realize that the words were just as important, if not more, than the pictures. My journey deeper into the world of scrapbooking started during this time; I decided to create an A B C book detailing Caleb's first year of life.

At the same time in my professional career, my second grade class had looped up to third grade with me. I had tons of pictures of them from the two years. In years past, we had created small photo albums with the pictures, or I had just returned them at the end of the year. I wanted this class to have a special reminder of their two years with me. So, I decided to have them make a scrapbook. Because of time and lack of knowledge, we still focused mainly on pictures and quick captions. It was a beginning.

Two things happened the next summer to convince me to begin researching better ways to scrapbook in the classroom and add lessons to my writing workshop, one a life-changing event and the other just a few short moments in the car. It was not long after I became a NJWPT/Abydos trainer and read *Aging with Grace* by Dr. David Snowden that I realized my grandfather had Alzheimer's. Through spending time with him, though, I saw a gift being given to me. He couldn't remember if he had eaten dinner on some days, but on other days he would sit and tell me story after story about his growing-up years and his time in the Navy and World War II, stories I had never heard before. I knew that I had to write these down so they could be kept and shared. My grandmother and I gathered pictures and began a scrapbook of his memories. Then, on the way home from their house one day, I heard a newly released song on the radio. The deejay said the title and singer, "Nineteen Somethin'" by Mark Wills, but I only connected with one chorus that first time, words about parachute pants and growing up. Memories from elementary school, like my friend Jason Davis and the many different colors of parachute pants he wore each day, came flooding over me. I'd not even thought of those years in forever, but it was so fun to look back and remember.

I started thinking about my students, who are about the same age as I was then. Will they remember those little things twenty years from now—the fads, the daily fun times with friends? We all seem to remember the big events, those indelible moments, like September 11, 2001, and the space shuttle disasters, but I began to see how the everyday moments were what I wanted my students to see and record as well.

I returned to my classroom with a desire to research ways I could guide my students through the scrapbooking process and help them write down the memories they were making. Each year, I have been able to change a few things, add more time and lessons in to the process, and see my students become excited about a new way of writing and recording.

Scrapbooking Minilessons From My Classroom

Many of my students don't know what a scrapbook is or do not have experiences with creating one. I chose this year to take some of the first time experiences that my third graders have had and use them as a frame for our scrapbooks. I begin the very first weeks of school sharing my favorite books. One of my favorite forms of writing is the ABC book, and I show the students my collection. I like ABC books because they can be multigenre and since our scrapbooks will cover the entire year together I want them to be multigenre as well. We decide our scrapbooks will be in the form of an ABC book, and we will add to each letter as we experience things we want to write about. I have already mapped out the year in my plans and have at least one focus for each letter. It will be the students' decision later whether to use my idea for the letter or one of their own.

The most important way for me to introduce a scrapbook is to show the students my own scrapbooks as well as to read books where the characters have a scrapbook such as *Zoe Sophia's Scrapbook: An Adventure in Venice* by Claudia Mauner. Because we have spent the first few weeks looking at the stages of the writing process, we can now connect the scrapbooking process to these stages as well. This is what my students have come up with:

> **Stages of Scrapbooking**
>
> Prewriting/Pre—scrapping (planning, looking at layouts, arranging the page and where everything will go, gathering tools they think they want to use)
>
> Drafting/Most of the time we write in our journal first and then choose what pieces if not the whole story, that we want to include on the page. We also sketch out what our page might look like.
>
> Revising and Editing/Besides revising and editing our writing, we also must look at if everything will fit, what pictures, stickers, or stencils should go on the page, and so forth.
>
> Publishing/This is when the page all comes together and we actually glue down and finalize our writing in color.

Just as in writing, my students immediately see the recursiveness of the scrapbooking process. Sometimes we arrange first and then write; sometimes we write first and then gather supplies for the page. It works either way!

Many of our "normal" writing minilessons fit in with our scrapbooking minilessons. From Barry Lane's, *Reviser's Toolbox*, I teach snapshots and thoughtshots, showing my students more ways to show, don't tell and prove it (74-75). In Nanci Atwell's *Lessons that Change Writers*, she shares Georgia Heard's idea from *Awakening the Heart: Exploring Poetry in Elementary and Middle School* of Heart Mapping (12). Atwell writes, "Georgia Heard suggests that we literally draw the place where our feelings reside; create maps of our heart and explore the territory of our feelings." (13) I read *Treasures of the Heart* by A.A. Milner as an opening. The students then divide a heart they have drawn into pieces representing the pieces of their own heart. I ask them to think of the people or things in their life that take up space in their heart and mean the most to them. They really think in depth and evaluate their priorities. This lesson generates prewriting ideas as well as generating a memorable page from this moment in their life (Fig 10.1). Atwell titles Lesson 11, *The Rule of Write About*

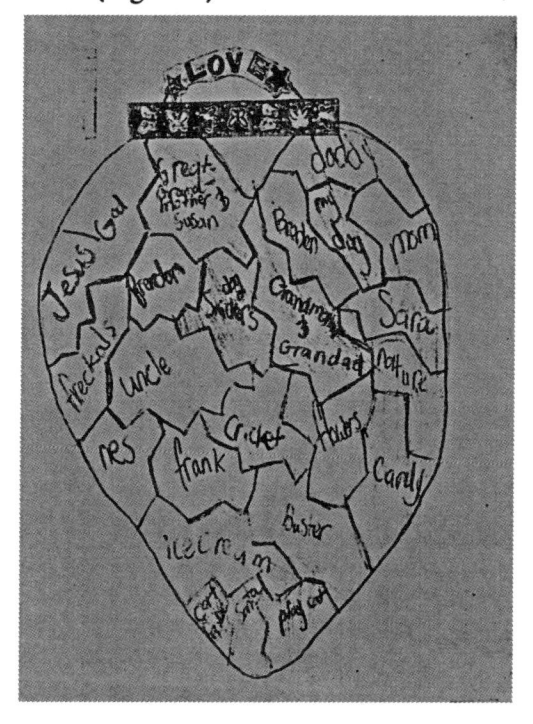

Fig. 10.1

a Pebble, or "No Ideas, but in Things." I use the Ralph Fletcher book, *Ordinary Things: Poems From a Walk in Early Spring*, to jumpstart the kids thinking about normal, everyday things they encounter. I want them to see what is around them as special even if it seems ordinary. An adventure doesn't have to be a trip to New York or a day at the amusement park. An adventure can be buying a new pair of shoes from the crowded store, walking through the park, or driving down the road on a foggy day.

"Visual literacy," or scrapbooking in the classroom, teaches the students to see their world in a new way and capture those moments through art and writing. Thus, this creates a life long reading and writing habit where students will have a memorable way to share their life stories.

11. Time is On Our Side

"Life is all about timing… the unreachable becomes reachable, the unavailable becomes available, the unattainable…attainable. Have the patience, wait it out. It's all about timing".
Stacey Charter

For my students and me, writing is now a joy not a struggle. It is a time of putting our most precious thoughts, our most vivid memories, our creative ideas, and all of the words we want to say down on paper. It is a time of reflecting, changing, and sharing. Writing is what builds the relationships in my classroom and makes the students want to stay awake until the very end of the day. Hopefully, I have provided ways for you to find and make the time to write in your classroom. You have all year to watch how starting a fifteen minute reading/ writing connection the first day turns into a day where the students haven't put down their pencils as you changed from subject to subject. It won't all happen at once, but it will happen—one writing day at a time. Your students will be asking you, "Is it writing time yet?" and you will be able to say, "Of course it is!" no matter what the time of day.

Appendix A—writing workshop Documentation Log

Dates: _____

Writing Conference Checklist

Name	Monday	Tuesday	Wednesday	Thursday	Friday
Aaliyah					
Joshua					
Kelsey					
Zachary					
Samantha					
Madison					
Karen					
April					
Christian					
Matthew					
Pattro					
Trent					
Emily					
Elizabeth					
Chad					
Samuel					
Jarrison					
Denicia					
Dillon					

Minilesson ideas: _____
_____
_____

Codes:
- ✓ Everything is going well.
- — The writer is struggling.
- Pa- Writing a story with a partner
- A - This child shared in Author's Chair.
- ✓+ The writing is surprising the writer and me.
- ♛ Keep in touch with this writer.
- ? I am not sure about their writing.
- P/I/T Publishing /Illustrating /Typing
- C - Conferenced with someone besides the teacher

References

Allen, Susan. *Read Anything Good Lately?* Minneapolis, MN:Millbrook Press, 2003.
Allen, Janet. *Words, Words, Words.* Portland, OR: Stenhouse Publishers, 1999.
Anderson, Carl. *How's It Going?* Portsmouth, NH: Heinemann, 2000.
Andreae, Giles. *Love is a Handful of Honey.* London: Orchard Books, 1999.
Appelt, Kathi. *Incredible Me!* NY.: Harper Collins Publishers, 2002.
Appelt, Kathi. *Elephants Aloft.* NY: Harcourt Children's Books, 1993.
Armstrong, Louis. *What a Wonderful Word.* Audio CD. NY: Verve Records. 1996.
Atwell, Nancie. *In the Middle New Understandings About Writing, Reading, and Learning.* Portsmouth, NH: Heinemann, 1998.
———. *Lessons That Change Writers.* Portsmouth, NH: Heinemann, 2002.
Bang, Molly. *When Sophie Gets Angry - Really, Really Angry…* NY: Scholastic, Inc., 1999.
Banyai, Istvan. *Zoom.* NY: Puffin, 1998.
Banyai, Istvan. *Re-Zoom.* NY: Puffin, 1998.
Baylor, Byrd. *I'm in Charge of Celebrations.* NY: Aladdin. 1995.
Bertram, Debbie and Susan Bloom. *The Best Place to Read.* NY: Random House Children's Books, 2003.
Blume, Judy. *The Pain and The Great One.* NY: Dell Dragonfly Books, 2001.
Brennan-Nelson, Denise. *My Teacher Likes to Say.* Chelsea, MI: Sleeping Bear Press, 2004.
Brennan-Nelson, Denise. *My Momma Likes to Say.* Chelsea, MI: Sleeping Bear Press, 2003.
Bridges, Shirin Yim. *Ruby's Wish.* San Francisco: Chronicle Books, 2002.
Brisson, Pat. *Beach Is to Fun: A Book of Relationships.* NY: Henry Holt and Company, 2004.
Brock, Paula. *Nudges.* Spring, TX: Absey & Co., 2002.
Brown, Margaret Wise. *The Important Book.* NY: HarperCollins Publishers, 1949.
Browne, Anthony. *Voices in the Park.* NY: DK Publishing, Inc., 1998.
Bruss, Deborah. *Book! Book! Book!* NY: Arthur A. Levine Books, 2001.
Bunting, Eve. *Smoky Night.* NY: Voyager Books, 1994.
Calkins, Lucy McCormick. *The Art of Teaching Writing.* Portsmouth, NH: Heinemann, 1986.
Carlson, Nancy. *How to Lose All Your Friends.* NY: Puffin Books, 1997.
Carroll, Joyce Armstrong and Edward E. Wilson. *Acts of Teaching: How to Teach Writing.* Englewood, CO: Teacher Ideas Press, 1993.
Carroll, Joyce Armstrong. *Authentic Strategies For High-Stakes Tests: A Practical Guide for English Language/Arts.* Spring, TX: Absey & Co., 2007.
———. *Dr. JAC's Guide to Writing With Depth.* Spring, TX: Absey & Co., 2002.
———. *Conclusions.* Spring, TX: Absey & Co., 2004.
Catalanato, Peter. *Emily's Art.* NY:Atheneum Books, 2001.
Cates, Karin. *The Secret Remedy Book A Story of Comfort and Love.* NY: Orchard Books, 2003.
Charbula, Barbara. *Before the Test: How I Taught Writing and Sixteen Out of Thirty-two Students Made the Highest Score: One Teacher's Narrative.* Spring, TX: Absey & Co., 2002.
Child, Lauren. *Beware of the Storybook Wolves.* NY: Arthur A. Levine Books, 2000.
———. *Who's Afraid of the Big Bad Book?* NY: Hyperion Books for Children, 2002.
Christelow, Eileen. *What Do Authors Do?* NY: Clarion Books, 1995.

Cleary, Brian P. *A Mink, a Fink, a Skating Rink: What is a Noun?* NY: Scholastic, Inc., 1999.
Clements, Rod. *Grandpa's Teeth.* NY: HarperCollins Publishers, 1997.
Couric, Katie. *The Brand New Kid.* NY: Doubleday, 2000.
Cowley, Joy. *Mrs. Goodstory.* Honesdale, PA: Boyds Mills Press, Inc., 2001.
Cronin, Doreen. *Diary of a Worm.* NY: Joanna Colter Books, 2003.
Crummel, Susan Stevens and Janet Stevens. *And the Dish Ran Away With The Spoon.* San Diego, CA: Harcourt, Inc., 2001.
———. *Cook-a-doodle-doo.* NY: Scholastic, Inc., 1999.
———. *My Big Dog.* NY: A Golden Book, 1999.
———. *Plaidypus Lost.* NY: Holiday House, 2004.
Cunningham, Patricia M. and Dorothy P. Hall. *Making Words.* Torrance: Good Apple, 1994.
Curtis, Jamie Lee. *Today I Feel Silly and Other Moods That Make My Day.* NY:Joanna Cotler Books, 1998.
Danneberg, Julie. *First Day Jitters.*Watertown, MA: Charlesbridge Publishing, 2000.
———. *First Year Letters.*Watertown, MA: Charlesbridge Publishing, 2003.
Demi. *The Empty Pot.* NY:Henry Holy and Co., 1996.
Degross, Monalisa . *Donovan's Word Jar.* NY: HarperCollins Children's Books, 1994.
dePaola, Tomie. *Strega Nona.* NY: Aladdin, 1979.
———. *The Art Lesson.* NY: The Putnam & Grosset Group, 1989.
Donnelly, Jennifer. *Humble Pie.* NY: Atheneum, 2002.
Dragonwagon, Crescent. *Home Place.*Minneapolis:Rebound by Sagebrush, 1999.
Duke, Kate. *Aunt Isabel Tells A Good One.* NY: Puffin Unicorn Books, 1992.
Edwards, Pamela Duncan. *Four Famished Foxes and Fosdyke.* NY: Harper Collins Publishers, 1995.
Falwell, Cathryn. *Word Wizard.* NY: Clarion Books, 1998.
Fitzhugh, Louise.*Harriet the Spy.* NY: Delacorte Press, 1992.
Fleming, Denise. *Alphabet Under Construction.* NY: Henry Holt and Company, 2002.
Fletcher, Ralph. *A Writer's Notebook: Unlocking the Writer Within You.* NY: Avon Books, Inc., 1996.
———. *Have You Been to the Beach Lately?* NY: Orchard Books, 2001.
———. *How Writers Work: Finding a Process that Works for You.* NY:Harper Trophy, 2000.
———. *Ordinary Things: Poems From a Walk in Early Spring.* NY: Atheneum Books for Young Readers, 1997.
———. *Poetry Matters: Writing a Poem from the Inside Out.* NY: Harper Trophy, 2002.
Fletcher, Ralph and Joann Portalupi. *Teaching the Qualities of Writing.* Portsmouth, NH: Firsthand, 2004.
Frame, Jeron Ashford. *Yesterday I Had The Blues.* Berkeley, CA: Tricycle Press, 2003.
Franco, Betsy. *Counting Caterpillars and Other Math Poems.* NY: Scholastic Professional Books, 1998.
Frasier, Debra. *Miss Alaineus: A Vocabulary Disaster.* San Diego, CA: Harcourt, Inc., 2000.
Freeman, Don. *Corduroy.* NY: Scholastic, Inc., 1968.
Friedman, Laurie B. *Back to School, Mallory.* NY: Carolrhoda Books, 2004.
Gwynne, Fred. *A Chocolate Moose for Dinner.* NY: Aladdin Paperbacks, 1976.
Harris, Wayne. *Judy and the Volcano.* NY: Scholastic, Inc., 1994.
Harvey, Stephanie and Anne Goudvis. *Strategies That Work: Teaching Comprehension to Enhance Understanding.* Portland, OR:Stenhouse Publishers, 2000.
Haseley, Dennis. *A Story for Bear.* San Diego, CA: Silver Whistle, 2002.
Henkes, Kevin. *Chrysanthemum.* NY: Greenwillow Books, 1991.
Heller, Ruth. *Many Luscious Lollipops: A Book about Adjectives.* NY: The Putnam & Grosset Group, 1989.
Hopkins, Lee Bennett. *Home to Me Poems Across America.* NY: Orchard Books, 2002.
Hopkins, Lee Bennett. *Marvelous Math: A Book of Poems.* NY: Scholastic, Inc., 1997.
Huliska-Beith, Laura. *The Book of Bad Ideas.* Boston, MA: Little, Brown and Company, 2000.
Jackson, Alison. *I know an Old Lady Who Swallowed a Pie.* NY: Dutton Children's Books, 1997.
James, Simon. *Dear Mr. Blueberry.* NY: Aladdin Press, 1991.
Johnson, Doug. *Substitute Teacher Plans.* NY: Henry Holt and Company, 2002.
Kilborne, Sarah S. *Peach & Blue.* NY: Dragonfly Books, 1994.
Kipfer, Barbara Ann. *1,400 Things for Kids to be Happy About.* NY: Workman Publishing Co., 1994.

Lane, Barry. *After the End.* Shoreham: Discover Writing Press, 1992.

Lane, Barry. *Reviser's Toolbox.* Shoreham: Discover Writing Press, 1999.

Layton, Neal. *The Sunday Blues A Book for Schoolchildren, School Teachers, and Anybody Else Who Dreads Monday Mornings.* Cambridge, MA: Candlewick Press, 2002.

Leedy, Loreen. *Look at My Book: How Kids Can Write & Illustrate Terrific Books.* NY: Holiday House, 2004.

Lester, Helen. *Author: A True Story.* Boston, MA: Houghton Mifflin Company, 1997.

Lovell, Patty. *Stand Tall, Molly Lou Melon.* NY: G.P. Putnam's Sons, 2001.

Lum, Kate. *What! Cried Granny An Almost Bedtime Story.* NY: Dial Books for Young Readers, 1999.

Lyon, George Ella. *Book.* NY: DK Publishing, Inc., 1999.

MacLachlan, Patricia. *All the Places to Love.* NY: Joanna Cotler, 1994.

———. *Sarah, Plain and Tall.* NY: HarperTrophy, 1997.

Marshall, Rita. *I Hate to Read.* Mankato: Creative Editions, 1992.

Martin, Ann M. and Laura Godwin. *The Doll People.* NY: Hyperion Books for Children, 2000.

Mauner, Claudia. *Zoe Sophia's Scrapbook An Adventure in Venice.* San Francisco, CA: Chronicle Books, 2003.

McDonald, Megan. *Judy Moody.* Cambridge, MA: Candlewick Press, 2002.

Mendez, Phil. *The Black Snowman.* NY: Scholastic, Inc., 1989.

Mochizuki, Ken. *Heroes.* NY: Lee & Low Books, 1995.

Moore, Helen H. *A Poem A Day.* NY: Scholastic, Inc., 1997.

Moss, Jeff. *The Butterfly Jar.* NY: Bantam, 1989.

Moss, Marissa. *Amelia's Notebook.* Middleton, WI: Pleasant Company, 1995.

———. *Max's Logbook.* NY: Scholastic Press, 2003.

Murphy, Mary. *The Alphabet Keeper.* NY: Alfred A. Knopf, 2002.

Newman, Leslea. *The Boy Who Cried Fabulous.* NY: Tricycle Press, 2004.

Nixon, Joan Lowery. *If You Were a Writer.* NY: Aladdin Paperbacks, 1995.

Numeroff, Laura. *If You Give an Author a Pencil.* Katonah: Richard C. Owen Publishers, Inc., 2002.

———. *10-Step Guide to Living with Your Monster.* NY: Laura Geringer Books, 2002.

O'Neill, Mary. *Hailstones and Halibut Bones.* NY: Doubleday, 1961.

Pearson, Emily. *Ordinary Mary's Extraordinary Deed.* Layton, UTY: Gibbs Smith, 2002.

Plourde, Lynn. *School Picture Day.* NY: Dutton Children's Books, 2002

Polacco, Patricia. *The Butterfly.* NY: Philomel, 2000.

———. *The Graves Family.* NY: Scholastic, Inc., 2003.

———. *My Rotten Redheaded Older Brother.* NY: Scholastic, Inc.,1994.

———. *Pink and Say.* NY: Scholastic, Inc.,1994.

———. *Thunder Cake.* NY: Putnam, 1990.

———. *When Lightning Comes in a Jar.* NY: Philomel Books, 2002.

Porto, Tony. *Blue Aliens: An Adventure in Color.* NY: Little, Brown and Company, 2003.

———. *Get Red: An Adventure in Color.* NY: Little, Brown and Company, 2002.

Poydor, Nancy. *First Day, Hooray!* NY: Holiday House, 2000.

Pulver, Robin. *Punctuation Takes a Vacation.* NY: Holiday House, 2004.

Ramos, Jodi. *Elementary Mini Lessons Lessons and Songs to Motivate, Inspire, and Improve Writing Skills.* Spring, TX: Absey & Co. 2000.

Rappaport, Doreen. *Martin's Big Words.* NY: Hyperion Books for Children, 2001.

Rattigan, Jama Kim. *Truman's Aunt Farm.* Boston: Houghton Mifflin Company, 1994.

Romano, Tom. *Clearing the Way: Working with Teenage Writers.* Portsmouth, NH: Heinemann, 1987.

Root, Phyllis. *The Name Quilt.* NY: Farrar, Straus and Giroux, 2003.

Ryan, Pam Munoz. *Hello Ocean.* Watertown: Charlesbridge Publishing, 2001.

———. *A Box of Friends.* Columbus: Gingham Dog Press, 2003.

Rylant, Cynthia. *Let's Go Home: The Wonderful Things About a House.* NY: Simon & Schuster Children's Publishing, 2002.

———. *The Relatives Came.* NY: Aladdin Books, 1995.

———. *When I Was Young in the Mountains.* NY: Puffin, 1982.

———. *The Wonderful Happens.* NY: Simon & Schuster Books for Young Readers, 2000.

Saltzberg, Barney. *Crazy Hair Day*. Cambridge, MA: Candlewick Press, 2003.
Seskin, Steven and Allen Shamblin. *Don't Laugh at Me*. Berkeley, CA: Tricycle Press, 2002.
Schotter, Roni. *Nothing Ever Happens on 90th Street*. NY: Scholastic, Inc., 1999.
Siebold, Jan. *Rope Burn*. Morton Grove, IL: Albert Whitman and Co., 1998.
Silverstein, Shel. "Little Abigail and the Beautiful Pony," *Where the Sidewalk Ends*. NY: HarperCollins Publishers, 1981.
Smothers, Ethel Footman. *The Hard-Times Jar*. NY: Frances Foster Books, 2003.
Snowdon, David. *Aging With Grace : What the Nun Study Teaches Us About Leading Longer, Healthier, and More Meaningful Lives*. NY: Bantam, 2002.
Steig, William. *Sylvester and the Magic Pebble*. NY: The Trumpet Club, 1969.
Steinberg, Laya. *Thesaurus Rex*. Cambridge, MA: Barefoot Books, 2003.
Stevens, Janet. *From Pictures to Words: A Book about Making a Book*. NY: Holiday House, 1995.
Suen, Anastasia. *Man on the Moon*. NY: Puffin, 2002.
Seuss, Dr. *Bartholomew Cubbins and the Oobleck*. NY: Random House, 1949.
———. *My Many Colored Days*. NY: Alfred A. Knopf, Inc., 1996.
———. *Gerald McBoing Boing*. NY: Random House, 1950.
Swanson, Susan Marie. *The First Thing My Mama Told Me*. NY: Harcourt, Inc. 2002.
Tang, Greg. *Math for All Seasons*. NY: Scholastic, Inc., 2002.
Taulbert, Clifton L. *Little Cliff's First Day of School*. NY: Puffin Books, 2003.
Teague, Mark. *Dear Mrs. LaRue*. NY: Scholastic Press, 2002.
———. *How I Spent My Summer Vacation*. NY: Crown Publishers, 1995.
Turner, Priscilla. *The War between the Vowels and the Consonants*. NY: Scholastic, Inc., 1996.
Van Alsburg, Chris. *The Mysteries of Harris Burdick*. NY: Houghton Mifflin, 1984.
Viorst, Judith. *Alexander and the Terrible, Horrible, No Good Very Bad Day*. New York. Scholastic, Inc. 1989.
Vizurraga, Susan. *Our Old House*. NY: Henry Holt and Company, 1997.
Waldron, Jan L. *John Pig's Halloween*. Bristol: Baby's First Book Club, 2001.
Walton, Rick. *Once There Was A Bull…(Frog)*. NY: The Putnam & Grosset Group, 1995.
———. *You Don't Always Get What You Want*. Salt Lake City: Gibbs Smith, Publisher, 1996.
Ward, Nick. *How to Be a Practically Perfect Pig*. NY: Scholastic, Inc., 1999.
Weiss, George David and Bob Thiele. *What a Wonderful World*. NY: Atheneum Books for Young Readers, 1967.
Whatley, Bruce. *Wait! No Paint!* USA: HarperCollins Publishers, 2001.
Wheeler, Lisa. *Porcupining*. Boston: Little, Brown and Company, 2002.
White, E.B. *Charlotte's Web*. NY: Scholastic, Inc., 1952
Willems, Mo. *Leonardo the Terrible Monster*. NY: Hyperion Books for Children, 2005.
Williams, Margery. *The Velveteen Rabbit*. NY: Doubleday Books for Young Readers, 1958.
Winch, John. *The Old Woman Who Loved to Read*. NY: Holiday House, 1996.
Wisniewski, David. *Tough Cookie*. NY: Lothrop, Lee & Shepard Books, 1999.
Wood, Audrey. *Quick as a Cricket*. NY: Scholastic, Inc.1982.
Wood, Douglas. *A Quiet Place*. NY: Simon & Schuster Books for Young Readers, 2002.
Wong, Janet S. *You Have to Write*. NY: Margaret K. McElderry Books, 2002.
Zinnser, William. *Writing About Your Life: A Journey Into the Past*. NY: Marlowe and Co., 2004.
Zolotow, Charlotte. *The Seashore Book*. USA: HarperCollins, 1992.